Angel Blessings

Angel Blessings

A magical collection of angel stories,
affirmations and creative ideas

JACKY NEWCOMB

A GODSFIELD BOOK

An Hachette UK Company
www.hachette.co.uk

First published in Great Britain in 2013 by
Godsfield, a division of Octopus Publishing Group Ltd
Endeavour House
189 Shaftesbury Avenue
London
WC2H 8JY
www.octopusbooks.co.uk

ISBN 978-1-84181-411-7

A CIP catalogue record for this book is available from
the British Library

Printed and bound in China

10 9 8 7 6 5 4 3 2 1

Contents

Introduction

Come and have fun with us, enjoy life and shine in our angel light

Welcome to my beautifully illustrated new book. I loved creating my previous book, *Angel Secrets*, and, as my readers asked for more ideas on ways to work with their angels, I couldn't wait to get started on this book, the second in the series. The minute I sit at my computer the ideas just flow onto the page, although of course you know that I've been helped – a lot! The angels certainly want you to awaken to their magical presence, so they are happy to help out in any way they can.

I have been researching and teaching people about angels and the afterlife for many years. I was excited by the way stories of angel intervention lifted people and made them feel safe and loved. I have made it my mission to share the best of these stories in my many books. Even if you haven't yet experienced an angel in your life, let me reassure you that angels exist – they are real.

Angels are beautiful beings of light, who are sent to Earth from the higher realms to help humankind on our life journey on Earth. Earthly lives can be challenging, and God sent his angels to assist us in whatever way they can. More and more people are becoming aware that angels are real. In 2008 an American survey discovered that 55 percent of Americans believe they have been protected by angels at some point during their lives. According to one youth survey (performed by Gallup), in 1994 76 percent of 508 teenagers (aged 13–17) said they thought angels were real beings. And in Canada another survey in 2008 revealed that 67 percent believed in the existence of angels. Other polls have shown that more women than men believe in angels; and the older you are, the more likely you are to believe they exist.

The tips and blessings in this book will help you connect to your own angel guides, and I know you will enjoy the stories as much as I've enjoyed sourcing them for you. If you have had an angel encounter, then you will know for sure that they exist; but if you're still waiting for one, you will be more likely to have some sort of encounter after reading about them. It's true! Many people write to tell me they have experienced their angels after reading one of my books, and I think it's because you know what you are looking for. Maybe it's also because you have a better understanding of what angels are, and you are less likely to be afraid of an encounter. Angels aren't meant to scare us, so this gives them the opportunity to leave you a sign in a safe and reassuring way.

Angel signs
Your sign might be the simplest of white angel feathers – a gentle and non-threatening way of letting you know that your angels are around you. Maybe your angel will appear in a dream (an approach often used by deceased loved ones, who appear to act in 'angelic ways'). Angels can hold your hand, or rest a reassuring hand upon your shoulder . . . And this is just the beginning. Each experience is received along with feelings of love and peace. These are encounters for us to enjoy. If it happens

to you, you'll realize how blessed you are, how blessed we all are! Look out for more ways in later chapters in which the angels can reach out to you.

I always suggest to readers that they make a note of any extraordinary angel moments they have, as well as recording how they feel about them at the time. Those brief encounters may be forgotten as we sit feeling sorry for ourselves about our challenging lives. I'll remind you over and over again to use your notebook and pen (or computer, if you prefer) to jot down those magical memories, ready to enjoy at your leisure as the years pass.

Although we never call ourselves psychics, my family has experienced psychic phenomena over several generations. Many of us have had premonitions and warnings of things to come. We have always put this down to the intervention of our guardian angels. Are we particularly lucky? Do we pay more attention to them than other people? I don't think so, but I wanted to find out. My research has meant that I've spoken to thousands and thousands of people who have experienced real-life angel intervention. I've learnt a few things on my journey, and of course I wanted to tell you all about them.

Angel tales and support

I have included some fascinating angel tales for you to enjoy. The experiences have come from my readers, posted from all over the world. Angels seem to have no barriers, and work with people of all religious backgrounds and those with no religious beliefs at all. Angels have no interest in our physical appearance, and they connect to our souls – the true part of who we are.

The angels' mission is simple. They bring us love and protection, watching over us until our earthly lives are through, whenever that might be. Angels are invisible to humans – at least most of the time – but don't think that means for one minute that they don't exist. They are with us in our hour of need, by our sides, when we need a little extra support and guidance. You might feel, sense or even hear them as they work to inspire you and whisper words of encouragement.

Mostly their messages come from deep inside, as a sort of inspirational thought. Have you ever wondered where your best ideas come from? Have you ever pondered how the perfect person walks into your life when you most need them, or the solution you have been looking for appears just after you 'ask' for it? When you're frightened and need support, someone often turns up. When you feel alone and call out for help, a friend will phone out of the blue. Angels have the ability to gently influence people to support each other. So if you feel an urge to reach out to someone, always follow your angel intuition. Your fellow human needs you too, so be an angel!

Angel rituals and figurines

You don't have to perform any type of ritual if you don't want to, but rituals can help, and they are also a lot of fun. Be involved as much or as little as you wish. I have a house full of angel figurines and angel-decorated products. I feel a sense of peace with them around me. This too might be something to which you're drawn – or not!

You can never have enough angels, in my opinion, and in my home angels sit on every shelf and adorn everything from plant pots to candleholders. Of course you don't have to spend a lot of money to acquire them. I have made some of mine; others I have picked up in sales (especially after Christmas) – just remove the holly and other seasonal trimmings and then you can keep them on show all year long.

Some of my favourite items have been found at charity shops and jumble sales. I can't resist taking these unwanted items home, for just a few coins. Or maybe friends will give them to you as presents. My collection has been built up over many years, but even one angel item can bring a little light into your relaxation space, or can be placed on a table next to the chair where you meditate or read.

How to use this book

You can read the book from start to finish, or dip in and out of it as you see fit. Because each chapter contains different sections of information, you can pick out all the true-life stories first and read them, for example, or all the angel blessings. There are no rules – only those that you make for yourself.

Many of the rituals and activities in this book require nothing more than a candle and a notepad and pen. Others require you simply to take time out in nature. There are plenty of ideas to choose from, so work with whatever inspires you.

Angel blessings

Angel blessings are thought-provoking sayings and suggestions relating to the lessons taught in the different chapters. These bits of inspirational advice are scattered throughout the book.

True-life stories

You can read extensively about angels, but nothing inspires as much as true-life stories – if it happened to other people, then it can happen to you too! The true-life stories in this book are real angel experiences from around the world, and I know you will enjoy hearing readers' tales relating to the different concepts that I've presented in this book.

Exercises

There are lots of ideas on ways to connect with your angels, ranging from meditations and manifestation rituals to activities using candles and crystals. Some of the exercises will be more exciting to you than others, so I suggest that you work with those that make your tummy flutter, and ignore the ones that don't seem so exciting for your personality type.

Affirmations

Affirmations are positive sayings that you can use to help you connect with your angels each day. There are affirmations at the start and end of each chapter in this book, and of course you can also make up your own.

Make angels part of your world

If, while reading this book, you have further questions that you'd like to ask, take a look at my previous book, *Angel Secrets*, which may well give you some answers. You may enjoy some of my other books too. If you have stories of your own that you'd like to share, you can post them to me in the special box on my website: JackyNewcomb.com.

My website also contains more angel stories for you to read. You can join my free mailing list there, or follow the links to my social-networking pages on Twitter and Facebook and interact with me live each day. You can also keep up-to-date with my book signings, personal appearances and workshops.

Create your own magical life, with your angels by your side. Feel their love for you – their human charges – every single day. And, like me, make angels part of your world by inviting them in.

I've loved creating this book for you. I hope you enjoy it too!

Angel blessings

Jacky Newcomb

Inviting angels into your life

We are with you, supporting your life choices, even if you don't sense us. Know that we are always around.

When you're feeling low, when you're sad and lonely, imagine if there was a big secret, a true and comforting fact: you are not alone. Every single one of us has an invisible friend. I'm not talking about the imaginary friends of children (although it's very possible that children's invisible friends are not imaginary). I'm talking about an energy of love that surrounds and protects you. The sparkle of light that you catch out of the corner of your eye – then you spin around and it's disappeared into thin air: you're experiencing your guardian angel, your close and perfect confidant, a being who loves you unconditionally.

Your angel is always around when you find yourself in trouble. Your angel finds real-life humans to assist you when you're feeling down. Your angel will help in ways that seem miraculous to us humans. Angels bring support in ways that appear to be coincidence, but really it's

'synchronicity' – that perfect blend of being in the right place at the right time for an ideal solution to occur.

Angels are a blessing ... an angelic blessing! They lift you up when you're down, lighten your load when it's too much to bear, and hold out a hand to support you when you need a companion. Angels always find a way of bringing light from darkness and good from evil, and their stories of protection are legendary.

Angels work in different ways

Each angel works in a unique way and, like teachers, each has its own distinct style. Some angels are quite hands-on and like to direct things in your life, while others prefer a more subtle approach. But angels never interfere, and their most important role is to help us to make the right decisions for ourselves. They prefer to let us work things out on our own and only step in once we've tried and failed at something. Of course this can be frustrating, but in the long run it makes sense.

Imagine you are running a special race, and you're fast – even though you trip over, you jump straight up and catch up, maybe overtaking the other runners and reaching the winning line first. You stand proudly on the podium to accept your winning certificate or trophy, knowing that you made it all by yourself.

Let's look at the same scenario, but this time when you fall your guardian angel picks you up and flies you past the finishing line. This might seem more fun, but in the end who won the race? Was it you? Or was it your guardian angel? We chose to live on Earth because of the amazing opportunities that we have to grow and learn, so let's learn from our own mistakes.

Now, I'm sounding a little mean. It's okay to ask your guardian angel for help – but help to solve the problem, rather than to handle every little detail for you. You must work it out with a few clues from your heavenly friends: they're ready, willing and able. Imagine your angel is cheering you on from the sidelines, encouraging you, or smiling and waiting for you as you cross the line ... Now that's the sort of support we could all do with.

What are angels?

The word 'angel' translates as 'messenger'. Angels are created by God (our Creator) as soldiers, messengers and protectors; their heavenly roles are those of praising and praying, and the worshipping of God. They also perform various tasks for humankind (at God's will), and these include: working with (and appearing to) the sick and dying; passing on messages; carrying information; guiding; and protecting.

There are many different types of angels, with both small and large responsibilities. We've learnt a lot about angels from the Bible, but they also appear in the Koran and other religious texts, in one form or another, even if they are given different names. Angels are intermediaries between the higher 'light' levels of contact and the lower human 'sound-energy' levels of communication. They sit between humankind and our Creator God and are able to reach down into our dense human space and help us.

Types of angels

There are many tiers of angels, but those that work closest to humankind are called guardian angels. They are the ones we feel, sense, smell and sometimes see. We each have our very own guardian angels; their role is to support and guide us during our earthly lives, to love, care for and protect us. Knowing that we are never left to flounder alone – that angels are orchestrating things from the higher realms – is such a wonder! These glittering companions adore us so much.

The New Testament mentions seven orders of angels: Angels (the lowest, or 'guardian angels'), Powers, Principalities, Dominions (or Dominations), Virtues, Thrones and Archangels. The Old Testament actually includes two others: Seraphs (or Seraphim) and Cherubs (Cherubim – not to be confused with the chubby cherubs that you see on Christmas cards). Cherubs are so integrated into our cultures however, that they appear on everything from art to architecture. Real or not, they will always have a place in our hearts!

Angel blessing

Angels around us, angels beside us, angels within us.
Angels are watching over you when times are good or stressed.
Their wings wrap gently around you,
Whispering that you are loved and blessed.

What do angels look like?

Angels are never described as 'cherubs'. The chubby baby images that we see on paintings and statues are a creation of humankind. Early civilizations lost many babies to a premature death and, in their mourning, chose to believe that their babies grew wings and became angels after passing over; cherub symbols were a great support to them. Yet there is no 'death' – or not at least in the way we traditionally view it. Millions of people have experienced a 'near-death phenomenon' when they find themselves leaving their physical bodies as their heart stops. But life continues once we leave our human shells, as many have come back to share with us.

When angels visit humans, they often seem to appear either as grown men (which are mistaken for humans) or as a paranormal vision. They have also manifested as glowing white figures or other unusual variations. For example, in the Bible, Daniel saw an angel that appeared to have a face that resembled lightning, and arms and legs that looked like polished metal and precious stones. There is nothing fluffy about that, is there? Maybe there is a difference between what angels really look like and how they choose to show themselves. Either way, they are happy with our human representations. Our paintings and statues remind us that the angelic race is real, and that can't be a bad thing.

Angels in dreams

This is such a big subject that I've devoted a chapter to it (see pages 146–173). My own angels love to appear in dreams. They visit me in this way, appearing not as glowing beings dressed in white with wings, but more as human souls, in all sorts of story-lessons. I awaken knowing the message behind the dream I've just experienced. Do your angels appear to you in this way?

Angel blessing

This is a traditional angel prayer.

Angel of God,
My guardian dear,
To whom His love
Commits me here,
Ever this day (or night)
Be at my side,
To light and guard,
To rule and guide.
Amen

Earth angels

An earth angel is an 'angel' that is currently living a human life. Such 'angels' may also include star beings, aliens/visitors, elementals (beings from the faerie realms), and so on. They are said to be incarnated beings who volunteer to be on Earth at this time of transition and change. Are you an earth angel? Many people feel they are.

Angel signs

So how do we know when angels are around us? How can we tell when they are close? Let's have a look at a few of the ways in which they let us know. Our angel friends leave signs for us everywhere we go ... we need only stay alert and ready.

Angels bring scents

Angels often show their presence by arriving on a cloud of perfume or flowery scents. This can happen when we're grieving or around the time of passing of a loved one. It's their way of saying: 'Don't worry, everything is in hand. We have control over the situation and your loved ones are here with us and safe.' Sometimes they can visit long after the passing of a loved one, and that beautiful puff of cologne means: 'Everything is well, we are here for you.' Their scent is a way of bringing us comfort.

Angels bring music

Angels can let us know they are around by giving us the privilege of hearing the sound of the 'angelic choir'. Imagine a thousand voices all singing in harmony – you can barely believe how amazing it is! Very few people hear the celestial orchestra, so if you are lucky enough to have this experience, know that you are honoured. It means that you are being supported and cared for.

Angels will sometimes announce their presence for the very first time by sharing their magical resonance – they do this when they are praising the supreme Creator God.

Angel blessing

Remember to thank the angels for sharing your life. When you sense them around you, when you feel their touch or hear their angelic music, for example, tell them: 'I hear you, I sense you … I smell your perfume – thank you, angels.' When the angels know that you understand their signals, they will repeat them for you.

Angels bring white feathers

People the world over search for white-feather gifts from their guardian angels. When you ask for an angel sign, discovering a white feather is the

most common response. You might find it in an obvious place, such as under a tree where birds gather, but your feather sign is more likely to appear in an unexpected or unusual spot. Many of my readers gather their angel gifts and store them in a special box or jar, or recycle their comforting feather signs by passing them on to strangers in need. You could do this too.

Modern-day angel signs

These days your angel may well send you a sign using modern-day equipment. It's not uncommon for angels to ring your phone, leave messages on your computer screen or play about with your mobile; they love to flicker lights and set off alarms too. Sometimes these little signs are all about timing. The reader in the story below felt that her vibrating phone was a way of stopping her in her tracks, just a little 'Hello, everything okay?' It doesn't need to be specific, and there are many signs like these that can have the same effect: the postman pops a letter through the door and it's from an old friend; your cat suddenly comes over for a fuss; or a cheeky bird taps on the window.

True-life story
Telephone call from the Other Side
Once, when I was really down towards the end of my marriage, I was on my own in the house, standing at the kitchen sink, crying my heart out. I was stunned into silence when I heard my phone vibrating on the coffee table in the lounge. When I went in, it was still vibrating, even though it was on silent; I picked it up, but nobody had called and there was no message.

Connecting with your guardian angel

Our angels assure us that we have no need to connect with them, because they are already in contact with us. But I think what we, as human beings, look for are signs that our guardian angels are around us; something tangible or physical that we can recognize as real-life contact. We are used to strong signs – things that are visual, audible or touchable; or at least something that we can smell (and occasionally taste).

Just this week I was chatting to my husband in a restaurant when I felt a hand resting upon my shoulder. The energy was comforting and friendly, and I spun around, half-expecting to see a relative standing behind my chair; when I looked, no one was there. In fact no one was even close to my chair, and my husband assured me that no living being had been near where we were sitting and he had a view over the whole restaurant.

Now you'd think that a touch like that – a spiritual touch – would be frightening, but it wasn't. Angels have to take care not to frighten their human charges, of course. An angel's kiss sounds wonderful, but not if it leaves you running screaming from the house. Can you see the dilemma? Angels have to sit on the fence between being gentle enough not to frighten us and strong enough that we notice their presence.

Asking for a sign

My favourite kind of angel contact is always an angel-feather sign, but I love dreams too. Why not ask for a sign yourself? Make a point of asking regularly each day: first thing in the morning or last thing at night perhaps. This is what you could say:

• My dear guardian angel, thank you for keeping me safe and watching over me each day. May I ask that you bring a sign of your presence today?

It's okay to ask your angels to keep a watchful eye on others too (if it's not appropriate, then they won't, so don't worry – just ask). You might change the wording to something like:

• My dear guardian angel and the angels of my loved ones, thank you for keeping them safe each day. May I ask for a sign that you are protecting them and watching over them?

You could even insert a specific name, if you wished.

Other ways to ask for help

There are plenty of other fun ways in which you can connect with your guardian angel: wearing a piece of angel jewellery, carrying an angel coin or token, or keeping a printed 'angel card' in your purse (credit-card-sized works well). There are such wonderful items in gift shops and on the internet (I even have a small selection on my own website from time to time). Many items have the words 'Protected by angels' printed on them, or angel images forming part of the decoration. Such inexpensive gifts are the perfect way to ask for angelic help. And of course you can always make your own.

Making an angel notebook

Often we miss the magic of everyday life; or if we do see everyday miracles, they get lost or forgotten in our busy lives. Why not make a note of them in a special way by recording them in a tiny 'travel-sized' notebook that you carry around in your pocket or bag?

Of course you can buy pretty little notebooks, but why not have a go at making your own? Pick up a few sheets of coloured paper (the palest greys, blues, pinks or lilacs seem to be particularly angelic colours) and cut them to the size you want. Then cut a piece of lightweight cardboard to wrap around the front and back. Why not write 'Protected by angels' straight onto the cover? You could use a metallic or felt-tip pen to make it extra-special.

Decorate the notebook cover using angel-inspired themes, pretty wallpaper (strong enough to form the cover), wrapping paper or images cut from magazines or greetings cards. Once you've done this, you can staple the whole thing together. Don't make your notebook too big and heavy – better to fill it up with your magical words quickly and then create a new one! Pick a pretty piece of ribbon to tie around the whole notebook and hold it shut, making the contents more private. (T-shirts and summer tops often have ribbon inside the garment at the shoulders, intended to hold the item on the hanger in the shop – if, like me, you cut these out, you can recycle the ribbon for your notebooks.) Simply glue the centre of the ribbon to the middle of the spine and let the ends hang free. When you've written your notes, tie the ribbon around the notebook in a bow to fasten it closed. It makes your notebook more special.

You could also wrap up your notebook in a square of fabric, or make a little pouch to put it in and keep it safe and protected; even a plastic sandwich bag would help to keep the cover looking nice.

Why not make some extra notebooks and give them away as presents? Try to record some magic every day: a positive 'coincidence', paranormal experiences, gifts of angel feathers, feel-good stories that people have shared with you, or poems and quotes that inspire you. There is a belief that the more you record your magical life experiences, the more such experiences you'll have. Let the angels know that you're listening, and have fun with your angel notes.

Exercise

Car connection

Did you know that you can tune into your guardian angel pretty much anywhere? But it does help if you can shut out the world around you, either literally or mentally. One place where many of us get to be alone is sitting in a car. Why not take the opportunity to connect with your guardian angel before you start your journey or when you reach your destination? Perhaps you could do this each day in the car park at work before you begin your day.

1 First, make sure you are parked somewhere safe. Lock the car doors too – that will help you to relax.

2 Sit for a few moments with your eyes closed. Take a few deep breaths: in through your nose and out through your mouth. Imagine the face of your guardian angel is right in front of you – you might see a face or simply a ball of light (either is fine).

3 Ask your guardian angel to bring you a message, or just to surround you with a healing and loving presence. Give yourself two or three minutes to do this, if possible (if there is any likelihood that you might fall asleep, set an alarm on your phone or watch).

4 When you feel ready, open your eyes. Open the window a little and make sure you are fully 'back' before you go on your way.

Your angelic connection will work just as well in the shower or bath. Don't let your location or living situation stop you from reaching out to your angels!

Angel blessing

What do we have to be thankful for? Our angels are a blessing, of course, but so is everything in the world around us. I would like to share with you some inspiring angel stories and magical ways in which you, my readers, can connect to your own guardian angel.

I want you to learn to see the magic in simple things: a plant in bloom, a newborn chick, the enchanting light of a candle flame. Many things can be magical, if you let them …

When you're feeling lonely, know that we are always with you. No trial need ever be carried out alone.

Angel healing

We are with you, helping to heal you, hugging away your aches and pains

Over the many years that I've done research into angels and the angelic realms I've heard many stories of angel healing: stories about people in physical pain who've had miraculous recoveries or just felt or seen an angel when they most needed help. Many angels offer comfort, and it's not uncommon to feel an angel standing behind you or resting a comforting hand upon your shoulder.

You can also call upon the Archangel Raphael, for he is God's angel of healing.

Archangel Raphael, the healer

Raphael's name means 'God heals', and he is usually pictured walking with a staff (or caduceus) entwined with a snake. He is also known as 'the shining one who heals' – through, or on behalf of, our Lord God or Creator. Ask the Archangel Raphael (Raf-A-El) to assist you whenever you need a little healing boost, either for yourself or for others. Raphael works with all of Earth's healers: doctors, nurses, therapists, and so on. And he can work with you too.

According to legend, Raphael's true name was Labbiel. God changed his name to Raphael after the archangel sided with God on the issue of creating humankind. Raphael is one of seven archangels who stand before the throne of God, and he can assist in both bodily and spiritual healing. In fact many 'alternative' or spiritual healers ask angels to join them each time they treat a client, and the Archangel Raphael is the obvious choice.

When you hold the hand of a sick friend, imagine Raphael pouring healing energy down through your head and out through your hand. Let the healing light flood into your friend's body, and imagine all sickness draining out into the earth below. Stop before you feel tired! If you do feel tired, it's because you are giving your friend support using 'your' energy. Go back to imagining the healing energy flowing 'through' your body into your friend, and not 'from' your body.

Archangel Raphael is a sage and a seer, and conveys healing both physically and emotionally by giving and receiving love. He first appears in the Book of Tobias, where he is disguised in human form as the travelling companion of the younger Tobias, calling himself 'Azarias, the son of the great Ananias'. Raphael is a seraph (part of the angel group known as the Seraphim), but is also mentioned as being a member of the Cherubim, Dominations and Powers – a busy angel indeed.

How to work with Archangel Raphael to create healing

First of all, you can ask angels to help you keep your aura strong. Your aura is the natural energy field that surrounds your body. In abused people (or those who are unwell) the aura is shrunken close to the body, or is ragged and full of holes, offering little protection from the outside world. In people who are well and healthy (and confident) it is big and fluffy, shiny and bright, smooth around the edges and hole-free.

Archangel Raphael's Associations

Item	Association
Candle	Green or yellow candles for ritual healing, or to place on your angel healing altar
Crystal	Emerald, malachite, agate, opal, yellow topaz or serpentine; you can also pick your own crystal from the many blue, clear, green or yellow stones available
Chakra	Raphael is said to take care of the spiritual healing centre of the body around the heart – the 'heart chakra'
Element	Air; use wind-chimes inside and outside your home to remind you of Raphael
Herb	Angelica; place angelica in a pouch and hang it by your bed
Patron	Of healers, therapists and doctors
Essential oils	Myrrh, palmarosa, rose, bergamot, geranium, sandalwood, helichrysum, mint (all types) and thyme; check a specialist book for safe ways to use these oils
Oils associated with air	Peppermint, parsley, geranium, galbanum, rosemary, helichrysum, melissa, tea tree, lemongrass and ylang-ylang

Exercise

Healing meditation

Many doctors believe that illnesses and 'dis-ease' begin in the mind. By relaxing your body, you open yourself up to healing from the highest angelic realms. There are many documented stories of people healing their own illnesses, so imagine what you could do with a little help from your guardian angel. Always use this angel treatment alongside your conventional medicines, for in the end the best medicine may be that provided by your doctor or specialist. Whatever works, your angel will guide you to try a wide variety of different things.

1 First, find a quiet place to sit. With practice, this could be pretty well anywhere, but initially it's probably best to find a quiet corner of the house where you won't be disturbed.

2 If you wish, play some relaxing 'angel'-type music without words (you don't want to sing along inadvertently). Make sure you are wearing warm and comfortable clothes, or place a soft throw/ blanket over your knees so that you don't get cold. You might also want to burn a candle – I suggest a small tea-light in a glass, for safety (make sure that your pets cannot knock it over while you are relaxing with your eyes closed – setting your house on fire is not at all relaxing!).

3 You can record your own voice saying the words in steps 4–33, ask a friend to read them for you or memorize them (more or less). Read really slowly – more slowly than you would think – and keep your voice nice and soft, to help with the relaxation process. When you feel ready, let's begin.

4 Start by closing your eyes, then concentrate on relaxing every part of your body. Relax … relax … With every word you'll feel more and more relaxed.

5 I want you to begin to notice a buzzing energy running through your body now, a pleasant relaxing energy that starts to filter down

through the top of your head and flood into every part of your body. Relax ... you are feeling more and more relaxed ... [leave a few moments here before beginning again].

6 Feel the energy massage your scalp – feel this now ... [leave a gap].

7 Feel the energy massage your neck [leave a gap].

8 Feel the energy massage your shoulders [leave a gap].

9 You are feeling relaxed ... more and more relaxed ... Relax now ... relax. Feel the energy massage your back, your chest, your whole body, down and down ... [leave a gap].

10 Your arms ... elbows ... wrists ... hands ... [leave a gap].

11 You are feeling more and more relaxed, and this vibrating energy relaxes every part of your body ... Relax ... more and more relaxed ... [leave a gap].

12 Feel the energy massage your pelvis ... thighs ... [leave a gap].

13 Your knees ... your calves ... your ankles [leave a gap].

14 Your feet ... [leave a gap – then talk really slowly and quietly as if someone had turned down your speed-dial].

15 You now feel relaaaaaxed ... from your head ... to your toes ... Relaaaaaax ... relaaaaax.

16 You feel your body begin to float slightly ... Feel this now ... feel this happening ... You are completely safe

and surrounded by the love of your guardian angel. Feel yourself float ... lighter and lighter ... lifting slightly off the bed now ... Completely safe and secure ... feeling happy and well ... More and more relaxed ... feel completely relaxed now [leave a gap].

17 You begin to become aware that your guardian angel is in front of you – a beautiful being of light – a being offering total, unconditional love ... Feel completely relaxed and at ease [leave a gap].

18 Feel happy and contented ... healthy and well. Your guardian angel is directing a healing beam of light along your body ... You can feel this working on your body right now ... and you're feeling completely relaxed, happy and well ... more and more relaxed [leave a gap].

19 As your guardian angel directs the beam of light around your body you can feel relief as any tension is removed. You know that the light is healing you, helping you ... relaxing you ... Relax ... relaaaaaax ... Enjoy the sensation and feel it helping you right now ... [leave a gap and then almost whisper the next words really slowly].

20 Feeeeel the beam of light healing your body ... healing ... heal-ing ... heal-ing ... Feeeel this now ... [leave a gap].

21 Know that this work is done by your own guardian angel with love ... unconditional love ... Your guardian angel loves you, exactly as you are, right now ... Healing ... healing ... healing your body, relaxing you ... Sending you unconditional love ... [leave a gap].

22 Direct the healing light into all the tense areas of your body: your spine ... [leave a gap].

23 Your shoulders ... [Leave a gap]

24 Your arms ... [leave a gap].

25 Ask your angel to target specific areas right now ... [leave a gap].

26 Right now ... you are in charge of this healing energy ... You help your angel direct it where you want it to go ... [leave a gap].

27 Feeling relaxed ... totally relaxed ... More and more relaxed ... Floating in bliss now ... feeling blissful, surrounded by total unconditional love ... Just float now for a few moments – just you and your loving angel ... all the while feeling completely safe and secure ... totally loved ... [leave a much longer gap here – several minutes].

28 Nearly done now ... [leave a gap].

29 And now it's time to come back into the room [leave a gap].

30 Thank your angel for your healing boost ... [leave a gap].

31 Remember that you can come back to this healing space at any time. But now it's time to come back into the room ... [leave a gap, then begin speaking more quickly and a little more loudly].

32 Open your eyes when you are ready. Spend a few moments bringing your consciousness back into the room. Stretch, if you want to – maybe have a little yawn [leave a gap, then speak more loudly and quickly].

33 You are now wide awake, wide awake ... Completely awake now ... and back in the room. WIDE AWAKE NOW. Smile!

It can take a few moments to get your body moving after this meditation. If you've been completely relaxed it's like awakening after a deep sleep. When you feel ready, you can stand up and have a little shake, reanimating your body. Maybe have a drink of water or a hot drink and a little snack (a piece of fruit or a biscuit). If you wish, you can write down your experiences in a notebook – or your angel journal. Date your entries, so that you can refer back to them. Recording all these experiences is very useful in learning from them.

Angel blessing

Thank you, angels, for your health and healing
Thank you, angels, for this magical feeling
Caring for my body in a partnership of love
My guardian angel sent from above.

How can angels help people in need?

Sometimes the greatest pain relief can occur through the power of the mind. I recall once sitting on a train with raging toothache. There were no other passengers, and I didn't have any painkillers in my handbag. Using a combination of Reiki healing (a sort of spiritual healing) and requesting help from my guardian angel, I began to relax. My body flooded with its own natural endorphins. Was this coincidence or angel power? You know what I believe, but who cares – it worked just fine. If you're ever in a situation where you need emergency pain relief, you might want to give it a go! This is what to do:

• First, ask your guardian angel to be present.
• If possible, hold your hands over the area in pain.
• Imagine (as in the meditation on page 32) that your angel is standing holding out his or her hands, directing a healing beam of light to the affected area.
• Relax and let it happen – feel the energy as it enters your body. Know it's real, and then just rest and let the angels do their work.
• Keep as still and relaxed as you possibly can – do not panic!

As soon as possible, get conventional treatment from your doctor or hospital. However, this angelic 'treatment' can be really useful in emergencies. If you encounter an accident and have telephoned the emergency services and done everything you can to help (or others are doing so), talk your 'patient' through the procedure – help them imagine they are being treated by angels. If you can't get close, or it's too dangerous to do so, follow the procedure in your mind. Ask the angels to attend the sick or injured person and, with their help, direct their healing energy towards the patient or to the specific area of pain or injury (if known).

Soothing words of comfort in challenging situations can really encourage someone to heal. If you tell them help is on its way and they are going to be okay, they probably will be! Afterwards don't forget to thank the angels for their help.

True-life story
Raphael's dental treatment

My young son and I were playing together one day when suddenly he accidentally hit his head against my teeth. It really hurt, and the doctor told me it had made my teeth loose. The pain continued for weeks and I was really frustrated, not knowing what to do.

Then one day the Archangel Raphael came into my mind. As Raphael is the angel in charge of healing, I wondered why I had never considered asking for his angelic help before. Almost immediately I felt Raphael's energy coming into the room. Right away I asked him if I could receive the strongest possible healing, to make my teeth like they used to be. Strangely I fell asleep right away! The very next morning the pain in my teeth had disappeared. I had no further problems with them at all, and they were completely back to normal.

Other inspirational stories

How have angels helped people in the past? The lady in the true-life story below had heart problems, so walking was a challenge for her. When she was abandoned without a vehicle, she believes the angels came to her rescue.

True-life story
Angelic help

Last week I needed a lift to collect my car from the garage. I was let down with the lift and had no money for a taxi and no credit on my phone. On my way to get some money for the mechanic I asked an angel to help me get a lift (money is very tight at the moment). Then a customer I knew from my shop came over to say hello. She asked me where I was off to, and I explained that I was taking the long walk to pick up my car. Then I heard the words I was longing to hear: she asked me to hop into her car as she was going exactly that way. After she dropped me off she sent me a credit for my phone, too! Thanks, angels.

More on meditation for healing

Some of the best healing experiences seem to come about when we are able to relax and let go of stress. The body has its own way of healing the body, and many of our ailments seem to be carried in (or on) the body as a result of stress. Meditation is a great stress reliever, and if you can sit down once a day for 20 minutes or so, close your eyes and relax, you can achieve amazing things.

At a recent mind/body/spirit event a couple of lovely ladies came over to chat to me at my book-signing table. They had attended my meditation session at the same healing festival earlier in the year. Both had had amazing experiences afterwards. One had been feeling pain in her legs, which disappeared after the session and never came back; the other had recently had an operation and was due for a second when she attended my healing session. Like her friend, she felt a 'shift' happen during the meditation and told me that her body had healed to the point where the hospital said she no longer needed the operation! Both felt that the angel meditation had been the key to their relief.

The point is that relaxation meditation does seem to help with healing. I know I hadn't done the healing personally, but perhaps my guided meditation (in which I gave suggestions under a light 'trance-type' meditation, that their angels were working on healing their bodies and releasing stress from them) did work.

There is nothing magical about what I do, and I'm sure there are many more polite people who have attended my meditation sessions and have had no experiences at all. To me the amazing thing is that we personally have so much control over our own healing, and in ways that we could never imagine. I suffer from the skin condition known as psoriasis, which has been linked to stress, and I know for a fact that when I am under pressure the condition gets worse. Many people tell me it's the same with eczema. Sometimes I can get my condition under control and at other times I can't – it doesn't seem to be an exact science, but relaxation time certainly helps.

Why not have a go at working on your own health and healing? You don't need to wait until you are actually ill. Always ask the angels to help you, then see if you can perform some little miracles of your own.

True-life story
Feather protection

I was due to go in for a big operation and was worried about it. For about two or three weeks beforehand I kept feeling a draught directly in front of me. It didn't matter where I went in my house – there it was. Then one day, while I was sitting on my sofa, a pure-white feather floated down in front of me. I knew then that my angel would look after me throughout my surgery and I didn't worry any more.

Healing gifts for friends

Many angel products are suitable as healing gifts for friends:

- **Little angel pin:** This is the perfect thing to attach to a dressing gown and wear in hospital.
- **Teddy bears:** Bears and other stuffed toys with angel wings are good for younger children, and some of them are even suitable for small

babies. These toys help to remind them that they are always protected by angels.

- **A book with angel stories:** A book like this one may be appreciated by older patients. The positive experiences of other people's angel contacts can be most reassuring and can make them more open to angelic intervention of the healing kind.
- **Angel greetings cards:** These make good get-well cards. You can also recycle Christmas cards and use them in this way, if you are good at crafts.
- **Carved angel crystals:** Such crystals are available in many crystal shops. Pink-hued rose quartz is a beautiful healing stone with loving qualities. You could present it in a soft fabric pouch, which can be kept in a spongebag as a gentle reminder of angelic presence.
- **Soaps moulded into angel shapes:** These are quite large, but everyone needs soap in hospital.

Look out for little presents like these and, when you see them, buy them to have ready as emergency gifts.

True-life story
Prayer protection

When my baby niece was born more than a month early she was very ill and had to undergo several operations. The family all prayed for her, and her mother said the baby kept looking up at the corner of the hospital ceiling and smiling. I like to think it was the angels healing her as a result of all the prayers we'd said.

Calling in angel help

Remember to tell a sick friend or relative that the angels are around for them, and remind them to ask that the angels draw close when they feel nervous or afraid. Many people have angel experiences following such requests when they are unwell and in hospital. Although I've been under general anaesthetic several times, I've never had an angel encounter in this way myself, but many of my readers have.

During recovery, angels (who sometimes appear as human souls) can often be seen sitting on the end of the bed or in the hospital visiting chair, or just popping in to reassure their human charges that they are not alone. Of course only the sick person is privileged enough to see them – usually!

The little voice within that reassures you that everything is going to be okay generally appears at this time too. When I was giving birth to my second daughter the midwife and nurse were rushing around trying to get emergency equipment ready, as the baby's heartbeat was dipping very low. I heard a reassuring voice in my head telling me that my baby was going to be completely fine and not to worry, so I didn't. Just as the voice had said, my little girl was born healthy and well, needing no medical assistance at all. The staff were impressed that I had kept so calm during the entire procedure – my angel was keeping me serene and composed right up to the end.

True-life story
Raphael's help

When I had an operation a few weeks ago I called upon the Archangel Raphael to heal the wound. It healed cleanly, and the infection that had been there before the operation disappeared. I also call on him every night, and occasionally at other times, to help with chronic pain.

Crystal first-aid box

If you love crystals and enjoy working with them, why not create a crystal first-aid box to use alongside your normal first-aid kit. You can give your 'patient' a crystal to hold (if it's safe and appropriate to do so).

Look for smooth-edged crystals, and buy them from a shop, if you can, rather than the internet (that way you get the opportunity to hold the crystals in your hand so that you can decide if they feel right). Smooth crystals and pebbles can be very calming. Round, oval and flat shapes are worth trying. Pick up a selection, if there is a choice, and hold them in the palm of your hand, then swap them from hand to hand. You will decide fairly quickly if a particular crystal (or pebble) is going to be helpful for healing purposes. A good book on crystals will help you. Select a few crystals to get started with, then add to them as time goes on (and finances allow). Over the years you will build up a large collection.

Keep a notebook with your crystals, and make notes as to when and where you used each one. Date your entries and write up the results. You can call on the angels to assist you in choosing your crystals too, if you are going for the 'random' method. Over time you'll find crystals that work especially well for you and your family. Your notes will help guide you, but trust your instincts too.

Healing crystal preparation

I keep my healing crystals in a plastic craft box divided into sections; a plastic toolbox might also be suitable. If you buy a divided box beforehand, you can use the sections as a guide to what size of stones to buy. It's harder to buy the crystals first and then find a box to fit them. You can also keep your crystals in a small pouch, or wrapped in pieces of velvet or silk to keep them safe (some crystals are soft and easily damaged). Before using them, ask your angels to purify and dedicate the crystals for healing use.

Exercise

Angel/crystal healing dedication

You'll need to gather the following items: your chosen crystals; some kitchen paper; incense (optional); a kitchen bowl (clear, if possible, so that you can see what you are doing); a bottle of spring water; a soft (non-fluffy) cloth for drying or a hairdryer.

1 Lay out your crystals on some kitchen paper. You can also light some incense if you wish.

2 Place the crystals one at a time in the bowl, which you have half-filled with spring water, then swirl them around. You need to work quickly, because some crystals are damaged by prolonged exposure to moisture. As you swirl them around the water, say the following words:
• Angels, please dedicate this [name your crystal here] as an object of healing for my first-aid box. Please infuse this crystal with your healing light.

3 Now dry the stones (be careful, if you are using a hairdryer, not to get your electrical equipment wet).

4 If you are burning incense, draw your crystals through the smoke as part of the purification ceremony.

5 Then pack your crystals carefully away until you need them.

Crystals and their healing properties

Each crystal has a different energy related to helping a different type of illness or area of the body. You can lie down and place the crystals on the area of the body in need or simply hold the crystal in your hands. Copy out the details from the box on page 46 on a piece of paper and add it to your first-aid box as a guide to which crystals work on which conditions; or simply go with your instincts. You can also ask the patient to choose a crystal from your box (most people will be drawn to a particular colour). Once you have dedicated your 'first-aid' crystals to their job, try not to use them for any other reason.

Rituals to cleanse and activate your crystals

Before your crystal comes into your possession it may have passed through many different hands. Even if you have dug it up yourself, it may still require a little work before you can use it. Cleansing it will remove

Selecting crystals for healing

Crystal	Traditional healing uses
Red crystal (carnelian, jasper)	Headaches, sunburn, high temperatures and minor burns, aches and pains
Clear quartz	Skin conditions, colds and flu, cuts
Amethyst	Cramps, panic attacks, stressful situations, hormone-balancing
Black crystal (such as obsidian)	Toothache, joint pain, broken bones
Moonstone	Women's issues, such as monthly cramps
Citrine	Backache
Lapis lazuli	Migraine (place the crystal on the forehead as well as holding it in the hand)
Amber, amethyst	General headaches
Jade	Calming the nervous system
Green aventurine	Fevers, stress and as a general tonic
Sodalite, clear quartz	High or low blood pressure, keeping calm
Angelite and (more recently discovered) angelinite	Calling in the angelic realm for more challenging conditions* (while waiting for medical intervention, for example); use alongside another crystal

* Caution: Never use crystals instead of visiting your doctor or calling for medical assistance.

any debris or unwanted energy. Then you should charge (activate) the crystal by preparing it for whatever its purpose is to be – 'jump-starting' it into action. Here are a few ideas for you to try.

First of all, literally clean your crystals and remove any mud, dust, oil, sand or other debris. You can add a little salt to your cleansing water, if you feel it needs some extra help. Salt has been used in purification rituals for many centuries.

Sunlight will recharge your crystals with ultraviolet light: lay them on a tray outside in the sunlight for a few hours (ensuring they are safe from animals and birds) – clear quartz really loves this treatment. Moonlight is another wonderful method of charging your crystals in a gentle way. On the night of a full moon place your crystals on a windowsill where they will receive the moon's full glare.

When you nominate a crystal for a role, it may need a little extra attention to wake it up, so activate it with an 'initiation' ritual of some sort. This might include holding it, moving it around in your hands, sleeping with it (under your pillow) or simply looking at it. Whisper words to your crystal, asking it to perform its task. Your 'intent' (your wish or 'will') is everything! Make your intent clear and precise: be happy and uplifted about the role you want your crystal to perform. Your state of mind needs to be in a good place when you perform this ritual (if possible, make sure that you are healthy when you do so; if not, ask a friend or family member to do the ritual on your behalf). Write your request on a piece of paper and place the crystal on top, to absorb the thought energy.

You can 'smudge' your crystal by holding it in the smoke of a sage wand/smudge stick or by moving it through incense smoke (Nag Champa and frankincense are both good) to cleanse/clear old energies from it. A smudge stick is a bundle of dried herbs, most commonly white sage (*Salvia apiana*), although other plants can be mixed with it (lavender, cedar, mugwort, for example). Native Americans used the smoke from bundles of dried sage (usually tied together with coloured threads) to clear the air of negativity and cleanse the air around a person or space.

If you are a Reiki practitioner or practise any other sort of healing, use that energy to recharge your crystals. If you want to have a go at this and are not trained in a specific healing art, simply hold the crystal in your left hand, with your right hand over the top. (If you are left-handed, do this the opposite way round – use your leading hand to bring in the energy.) Imagine the universal life-force energy pouring down through your head with the help of your guardian angel, and out through your hand into the crystal, in exactly the same way that you would channel healing to a person. You may well feel warmth as this happens. Once you sense the energy has stopped flowing, you know that your crystal has been charged sufficiently.

Perform these rituals every few months or so, depending on how often your crystals are used. If the stones are used for protection or healing purposes, they gather up negative energies like a battery. Regularly clear and cleanse, activate and charge the crystals in your collection, whenever you feel the need.

Healing pebbles

A beach pebble is a useful addition to your desk or to place beside the telephone, especially when you have difficult calls or letters to deal with. You can also add it to your crystal first-aid box. Next time you are near a beach, see if you can find a healing pebble. You'll notice that you are instinctively drawn to them. The ones I'm attracted to are smooth, round-edged and shallow, sometimes with a gentle indentation on the top – something you want to play with in your hands.

I like to keep a healing pebble in my car, shut away in the glove box when I'm not using it (if the car is involved in an accident, the pebble could become a dangerous projectile, and the idea is to help healing, not cause harm).

If you have to wait in a queue in your car (at a petrol station, for example, or waiting for the car wash), it's amazing how anxious you can become. Holding, smoothing and stroking your pebble will immediately restore peace and calm, relaxing you as you handle it. Sounds too good to be true? Give it a go – it won't even cost you any money to acquire one, just a little (fun) time on a beach or riverbank. A friend might appreciate a beach pebble too, especially if they were unable to join you on your trip – it makes a lovely souvenir. Hand it over with a note explaining where you found it, what it's for and how to use it.

True-life story

Angelic voice

I was receiving healing last night and I had my eyes closed. In my mind I saw what looked like an angel; he was so tall, and had lovely blue eyes and a long grey beard. He whispered to me 'Everything will be all right' in the softest voice. It was something I will never forget.

Thoughts are things

In the Christian tradition the 'Word' relates to Creation. Words create things. Sound is energy vibration, which floods through our bodies as we speak. As we've already discussed, a lot of healing comes about because of our belief. We can help create a state of wellness by the thoughts that we think and hold. Watch the words that you say aloud – and even the thoughts that you think. Remember: thoughts are things. So if you constantly use negative phrases, don't be surprised if what you say manifests in your own body. Below are a few examples.

If you are constantly saying things like, 'I feel I am carrying the weight of the world on my shoulders', don't be surprised if you get shoulder ache. And how about:

• 'I wish you'd shut up – you're giving me a headache' (I bet you constantly get one!)

- 'You're a pain in the neck'
- 'You drive me crazy' (are you acting strangely now?)

See how it works? It seems obvious, once you know. Now that I've pointed it out, I bet you can think of many similar phrases that you use yourself. Ask the angels to help remind you each time you say these things, and try to use more positive words instead. For example:

- 'It really makes me happy when you … [add detail here]'
- 'I love it when you laugh/help around the house/are so supportive of my work [adapt as necessary]'

Change your thoughts in order to change your health – simple!

Healing angel feathers

The ancient philosopher Plato believed that the soul had to be healed before the body, and many other ancient traditions agree. The word 'disease' splits to indicate that we are 'dis-eased' – or ill at ease. There are many disciplines that can treat the emotional body (or the layers of the aura/energy body).

The body is surrounded by an egg-shaped energy field, known as the aura. When this is healthy (and you are fit and well), this energy field is full, fluffy and smooth, expanding a long way out from your body; it acts to protect you from negative outside influences. You can use your angel feather to fluff the aura back out again when you are unwell. While you perform this exercise, know in your mind that it is working – believe it to be true.

If you want to have a go at using a healing angel feather, first you'll need a large feather – you'll probably find one somewhere that large birds gather (by a pond or lake, for example); alternatively, search for a smudging feather from your New Age supplier (a large feather that usually comes with a handle, and is bound with leather, silk or ribbons – sometimes decorated). Before you use your feather, dedicate it to angel healing simply by asking permission from your angels to do so:

- Angels, please work with this feather to cleanse and clear my [or add someone else's name here] aura. Make my [their] energy field (aura) healthy and strong, shiny and bright. Thank you, angels.

After each use, cleanse the feather by drawing it backwards and forwards through the smoke of an incense stick or sage wand a few times.

Exercise

Cleanse your own aura

1 Ask your angels to assist with your aura work.

2 Stand and, using your feather, start by wafting out your energy field from the top of your head: push the energy outwards.

3 Work down your entire body (both front and back), wafting the feather away from your body and pushing it outwards to the length of your arms and legs – flick it out and imagine the protective aura layer expanding outwards from your body. See your aura as a thick, white, healthy, shining layer (like a fluffy cloud).

4 Now take the feather and, starting at the top of your head again, work an arm's length from your body, smoothing around the 'imagined' new outline of your aura. Work the front and back of your body, and then seal it all around by touching the ground with your feather.

5 When you feel you have completed your task, remember to thank the angels for their help.

Exercise

Cleanse a friend's aura

If you are working with a friend, take it in turns to perform the ritual.

1 As before, ask your angels to assist with your aura work.

2 Ask your friend to lie down on their back on a bed or healing table (or a soft rug on the floor). Starting from just above their

head, make flicking movements outwards with the feather to about an arm's length around the body.

3 Go backwards and forwards across the body, touching the floor with the feather on each side.

4 Then, working about an arm's length from the body, smooth the new 'imagined' outline of the aura all around them with the feather, until you instinctively know it has been done. Seal it all around by touching the ground with your feather.

5 Once you've finished the area around the feet, ask your friend to turn over so that they are lying on their front. Work on the other side of the body, following the instructions given above.

6 Thank your angels and swap over, so that your friend works on your aura in the same way.

Other things to do and make

There are various things you can do and make to give angelic healing a little boost.

Visualizations

If you want to be healthy and fit, a visualization helps a lot. Start by creating a montage of images that reflect your dream of yourself: find photographs or images cut from magazines of people exercising, having fun, relaxing on the beach, and so on. Add photos of healthy foods and images of yourself when you looked the way you wish to look now. If you've never yet looked the way you want to look, use photographs of yourself smiling or looking happy. If you don't have images like this, go and get some taken promptly!

Frame your montage, or at least stand it somewhere you'll be reminded of your goal every day. Don't forget to add the picture of an angel, and to ask your guardian angel for help in achieving success. Challenges are always easier when faced with a friend. Your angel's help is unconditional but remember to give permission for them to help you.

Salt-water cleansing

Cleansing your body in a salt bath can bring great benefits. The Dead Sea is so full of salt that you can only float in it, not swim! If you suffer from rheumatic pain or muscular aches, bathing in salt water helps to draw out impurities from the body and thus reduce the pain. Salt cleanses through the skin, using the natural process of osmosis; it also acts as an anti-inflammatory.

Why not have an 'angel detoxification bath'? Place an angel statue or figurine at the end of your bath, and next to it a sweetly scented aromatherapy candle (or two) of your favourite scent. For this ritual use Epsom salts (magnesium sulphate, which creates a static electrified field in the water, helping to draw impurities from the body). Put about 450 g (16 oz) of salts into the warm water and soak for around 20 minutes. Relax for an hour afterwards – my skin was soft for days after doing this treatment. Drink lots of water after your bath (this helps to speed up the process).

While you relax, ask your angel to assist you, as always. Strangely enough, many people have angel visitation experiences while bathing or showering, and maybe you will too. The more you relax, the more likely this is to happen. Enjoy!

Candle-making

Candles are used so much in angel rituals – why not have a go at making your own? Search the internet for details, or look for a boxed set that will contain everything you need. You can buy special shapes in which to mould your candles: choose angel shapes and create candles specially for your healing rituals. Add colours and aromatherapy oils (following the directions in your candle-making kit). You can even hand-carve magical symbols onto your candles if you are feeling really creative!

Things to do and make with children

Children like to be kept busy. A sick child off school is a bored child, so why not give him or her some angel activities? Vary the activities depending on the age or abilities of the child. Here is a selection of ideas to suit different personalities and why not join in too? Have a look through the list and see which of these ideas jump out at you.

Crystal fun

If age-appropriate, a basket of
smooth-edged crystals can be fun
to play with in bed. Encourage children
to make patterns or to sort the stones into
colours or shapes. Of course you are sneakily
passing on the healing abilities of the crystals at
the same time. After use, cleanse them by passing
them briefly through water and then incense (see
page 47).

Angel cards

If the child is well enough, why not create some
angel cards together, featuring positive sayings?
Cut up some old greetings cards (using an old
credit card as a template). Then come up with
some positive sayings together – your child can
write the phrases onto the card directly, or a
younger child can copy the words you have
written. You could even type up your phrases
on a computer and cut them out, for the child
to stick on to the card. Place the sayings on one
side of the card, and ask the child to illustrate
the card with pictures of his or her own angels on
the back.

Some suggestions for positive sayings are as follows
(keep them simple, short and something to which the
child can easily relate):

• Your angels are always with you
• The angels are taking care of you today
• Ask your angel to help you when you feel sad
• Your angels are your friends
• Angels can take care of your pets, if you ask them to
• Your angels want you to smile and be happy
• Your angels love you, like you love your family

- Your angels like to help you at school
- Your angels help you to eat healthy food
- The angels are with you when you sleep
- Your angels love it when you are kind to others

Ask your child to help you make up some more sayings. Ask: 'What do the angels do to help us?' When you've finished you can put the angel cards into a fabric bag or basket, then ask your child to pick out a card when he or she feels the need for a little support. Alternatively, why not pick out a card together at bedtime as part of your usual routine?

Angel stories

Why not suggest that your child writes a story about going on a magical journey with his or her guardian angel? Hand over a lined notebook and pen, then read out the following to inspire your child:

- One day [add child's name here] was at home poorly when his/ her guardian angel came to visit. 'Why don't we go on a magical adventure today?' the angel asked. 'By the time we get back I know you will feel much better.' [Child's name] agreed and his/her angel took him/her by the hand and they flew together up into the clouds and the adventure began ...

Then ask the child the following:

- What do you think happens next?
- Where would you go with your angel?
- What does your angel look like?
- What is your angel wearing?
- What is your angel's name?
- Why don't you carry on writing the story for me?

If your child is unable to write, then he or she might be able to draw some pictures to illustrate the adventure, or just tell you the story as it unfolds. What a fantastic way of inspiring their imagination! Of course your child's guardian angel will be looking on and helping with the healing.

Dressing up

Why not create a dedicated dressing-up basket for your child? Old lace curtain panels, threaded with elastic, unwanted petticoats, and anything shiny and sparkly is appropriate. You could incorporate shop-bought angel wings or wigs (available in many supermarket shops these days), or even mix it up with fairy wings and wands!

Sparkly scarves and lengths of glittery fabrics are a useful addition to your box; check out jumble sales or charity shops for more inspiration. Just remember to wash everything first. Card shops and fancy-dress hire shops will often stock feather boas; and maybe you could enlist the help of a favourite aunt or grandmother who might enjoy creating some fun angel clothing with their sewing box and secret stash of sparkly buttons and old sequins. Old rope tie-backs with tassels can make wonderful 'belts' to hold everything together!

When you feel unwell, relax and let us heal you. Be ready for the healing vibrations that we wash over your body.

Decorating with angels

Allow us to fill your home with our ever-loving light

Adding a few angel items around your home can help to create the most wonderful atmosphere. I have stacks of them, and people always comment on how welcoming the house feels when they enter. The first thing you see as you enter my door is an angel draught-excluder – now I have to confess that I don't have a draught at the door of my modern home, but the long, fabric-covered sausage-shape was so pretty with its row of cherubs that I had to have it anyway!

There are angel pictures hanging on the wall in the entrance hall, and my largest angel figurine sits on a waxed pine desk located under the stairs. Of course I have angels sitting outside the front door too; I forgot to mention them! Angel statues nestle each side of the entrance, half-hidden by pots of flowers and herbs, so that no one is in any doubt that they have reached the home of the 'Angel and Afterlife Lady'. Don't forget to hang up some outdoor 'faerie lights' for a little extra magic outside your own home – and a wind-chime for that exquisite sound each time the wind blows. My chimes are white, with inspirational messages inscribed down the side of them. Search out your local garden centre or architectural salvage yard for more fabulous finds, or experiment with painting items you already own.

Angel blessing

Our angels are always with us, but why not ask them to draw close to you when you are in your home? Ask that they fill it with the highest vibration of light energy. When you step over the threshold at the end of a challenging day, you'll feel a wonderful sense of angelic peace and love. Your home is your sanctuary, so ask the angels to help it stay that way.

Angel altars and other displays

I love angel altars and have mentioned them in many of my books. An angel altar is just a display of your favourite angel items. It can be a place where you sit and meditate or simply somewhere that you enjoy looking at as you pass by.

Your angel display can be created for a specific purpose or just as a pretty arrangement. I have several angel arrangements in my home at any one time. Below are a few examples of things you could try.

Fabric angels

You could put a fabric angel nestled amongst your china on a shelf in the kitchen. I have pretty shelves with plates, cups and saucers in different styles; the angels sit between the china and peep out over the teacups. They were specially designed to hang on a Christmas tree, so some of them have cotton loops that I hang on the cup hooks. I have a similar connection to faeries (nature's angels). One display of mine has faerie prints for extra impact.

Protective angels

Many years ago I started a tradition of using household putty to secure a tiny plastic angel over each doorframe. The children did this when they were young too. And I love angel plaques that say things like 'Protected by angels', and have them hanging together on the wall (some of my collections are featured on my website, if you want to take a look).

Angel rainbow crystals

One of the curtains in my angel room (my study, where I write my books) doesn't close because the pole is wrapped around with silk flowers, clip-on sparkly butterflies (many of which are made from real feathers) and angel rainbow crystals. The crystals hang in the window and create rainbows around the room. You can purchase many different styles – naturally, mine are all decorated with different types of angels. Maybe I should attach a curtain pole to the wood on the inside of the window and decorate that; then I could close the curtain at night! By the way, butterflies are angel signs and will often appear after you have asked for a sign from a deceased loved one or from your own guardian angel.

Other angel items

I collect angel-decorated items of all types (mainly plain cream or white, or gold versions). You don't have to spend a lot money (or any) doing this, if you want to join in the fun. Ask for angel items as birthday gifts, or look out for items in sales (especially after Christmas), car-boot or yard sales, jumble sales and charity/thrift shops. Garden centres are great places to hunt for angels – look in the 'reduced' sections. A Christmas angel whose snow is falling off is perfect for you to place in your home as a decoration all year round. Call in regularly to your garden centre; after a while the sales assistants may even put things by for you and bring them out when you return.

Angel books

I collect angel books in the same way. Many are second-hand (resale) items from charity shops, fetes and internet bookstores. You can pick them up for a fraction of the original cost and, of course, you can borrow books from your library. Let's keep this precious resource going, by supporting the library system.

True-life story
Angel-figurine sign

I was feeling really down one day. It was 11.30 at night and I was in on my own in my bedroom. I sat on my bed praying, and I was playing with my angel cards, a recent purchase. Mad as it sounds, I was chatting to my angels. I asked them for a sign to let me know they were around me and to give me a little comfort.

I collect angels and I have some beautiful ones, including some that light up when you turn them on. This particular day, when I asked for the sign, I requested that it would be a sign that I'd definitely recognize as being just for me. As it was 11.30 and I had work the next day I decided to try and get some sleep. I walked over to my lamp to unplug it and, out of the corner of my eye, I could see something shining. It was one of my angel figures. I nearly jumped out of my skin because it lit up all on its own! To be honest, at first I was a bit scared, so I turned all the lights on and sat on my bed, feeling petrified.

After a couple of minutes I calmed down and picked the angel up. It was definitely turned off at the switch, but I knew it would be. These angels are kept high up on some shelves above my bed, so I never really light them up. I was amazed, and so grateful for the sign because it was just what I needed.

I thanked the angels and lay in bed, and all the while I kept popping my head up to have a look at the angel – it was still lit up!

Angel bowls and cards

I have bowls (angel-decorated bowls, of course) on my desk containing an ever-changing arrangement of angel cards. My favourite are the angel-secrets cards I have designed myself. You can display them in their pretty box along with your angel books (look out for plate stands, so that the front covers face forward on your shelf or table) or, like me, keep the cards in an open bowl or basket so that you remember to use them every day.

Mini angel items

An old wooden printer's tray, or what we used to call a 'shadow box' (wooden shelving with tiny sections), is a great place to show off a mini-collection of angel-inspired items. Look out for angels carved out of

semi-precious stones (crystals) – you'll find these at gift shops, online and at healing-type fairs (try the crystal stall). In my collection I also have a pretty gold mini-angel, which was part of a broken key-ring. Keep open-minded when searching for treasures. At an antique shop once I found two precious angel brooches, one of which was made of pewter. Gift shops sell tiny angel figurines for pocket-money prices, so they're great for children.

Angel coins

I also collect angel coins. Numerous companies press these metal discs (not always round and coin-shaped) with angel shapes and angelic messages. I have bowls of assorted crystals around my home, and each one contains an angel coin (the angel connection helps to boost the energy of the crystals). Angel coins also make wonderful gifts for people, so it's worth carrying a couple around in your purse. You never know when you might be glad to give away this tiny sign of comfort and protection.

Angel candleholders

I have many angel candleholders too. A vast selection of these is available because they have been made for many years as Christmas decorations. Some of mine are new and suitable for tea-lights, while others are older and fit taller candles. I've never paid more than a small amount of money for any of them, and they are a useful addition to any angelic display in your home. Naturally, if you are craft-minded, you can make your own. Imagine the fun of moulding an angel candleholder in clay (look out for air-drying clay, as it's especially suitable). You could even add wings! Some of mine are spray-painted to match my mirror.

Angel stationery

My desk holds a collection of angel stationery: angel stamps (with gold stamp pads, so that I can personalize envelopes and notecards), angel journals, angel-decorated notebooks, a pen with angel wings (a new addition) and angel-decorated bowls and dishes for pins, paperclips and elastic bands. Naturally my wall clock has an angel on it too, and I have matching angel coasters on my desk for my water glass.

Angel gifts

Most recently I've added an angel-decorated tile – a gift (like many of my items) from a lovely fan. Fans have bought (and made) me the most exquisite items over the years: a crystal wand, angel pictures, knitted and crocheted angels, angel chimes, jewellery, dream-catchers and rainbow crystals, to name but a few. Thank you.

Crystal balls

One of my display areas is a glass shop-fitting type of unit, which is lit from above – an inexpensive display from a Swedish company. The glass shelves do need to be washed occasionally to keep them sparkling clean, but it's the perfect place to keep my most prized collection. I also collect crystal balls (mainly glass crystal of all sizes). The late fashion designer Coco Chanel had some in her Paris apartment, and when I saw a photograph of this when I was a young woman I was immediately inspired to make my own collection. Many of my crystal balls are on angel stands (actually the biggest one is held on an old aromatherapy oil-burner stand, recycled after the glass bowl at the top smashed).

Some of my glass globes have angels etched in the middle; another is etched on the side so that the ball reflects wonderful rainbow colours under the light. If you decide to collect crystal balls too, make sure you don't stand them on a windowsill. This is where the old wives' tale originated about crystal balls being dangerous – sunlight can concentrate the light in the glass and could create a fire in your home. I (stupidly) used to keep my collection in a conservatory. One day the sunlight from above actually burnt two holes in a wooden box that I had displayed next to the crystal balls – luckily, there was no actual fire! Collect these beautiful objects, but do display and treat them with respect.

More ideas for your displays

- Place displays on a pretty tablecloth. Keep it fresh, clean and ironed: tablecloths used for displays will need washing every few months, as they can collect dust. Enhance old cotton cloths by starching them in the old-fashioned way.
- Put a vase or pot of fresh flowers with your arrangement to add life-energy (dried and silk flowers, although pretty, are a bit lifeless). Refresh as necessary.
- Add angel figurines, books, cards and other angel-decorated objects to your display.
- Include a few pretty crystals, shells and feathers (white angel feathers, of course).
- Place a candle or two on your altar (natural-scented aromatherapy candles are perfect). If you can find holders decorated with angels, so much the better.

Your displays can be placed pretty well anywhere: inside (on a table, shelf, cupboard top or mantelpiece) or outside (see pages 70–76). You can have one large display or several smaller ones throughout your home or around a room. If space is tight, place your displays on the wall (as pictures or plaques) or on tiny shelves. Angel books can be stacked up by your favourite chair or placed in a basket on the floor. I love baskets, and use them everywhere and for everything.

If you meditate or relax in the same chair, you could stack up some prettily decorated hat boxes and keep your angel cards, books and other angel tools inside. Why not have a go at lining and covering some old shoeboxes with recycled wallpaper or wrapping paper? You can mix many patterns together, as long as you stick to two or three main colours. Work with flowers, stripes, spots and checks.

True-life story
Angelic advice

I have angels in all forms in just about every room in my house, including one in the bathroom, a sun-catcher. I ask my angels to help me when I feel I need them, but I know they are always listening. I also have a book by

*the side of my bed, and every now and then I ask the angels a question,
then open the book at random and read whatever I turn to on the page, to
see what advice my angels are giving me.*

On the road

For your car there are bumper stickers declaring 'Protected by angels'
and other comforting phrases. I love the one that states 'Never drive
faster than your angel can fly' – wise words indeed. You can purchase
an angel key-charm or key-ring to take care of your house and car
keys, too.

When travelling

Put an angel coin in your pocket, add an angel pin to your jacket or wear
a piece of angel jewellery when you are travelling. Put angel stickers on
your suitcase (not easy to find, I'll admit) or draw an angel and place it
behind the plastic of your address label on your bag to protect you (an
angel feather would serve the same purpose).

Ideas for your angel garden

You can create natural areas in your garden that are perfect as a
meditation spot, especially if you place a seat, bench or old log in a
corner space. Angel statues are lovely, but pricy. Keep an eye out for
house clearances (where agents or family sell off items after someone has
died). You know those much-loved items require a new home, and you'll
probably pick them up for a bargain price. Put in a request for angel
figurines on one of the recycling websites too; if you don't have one that's
based close to your home, consider setting one up.

I collect heart-shaped pebbles from nearby beaches – just one from
each beach! Take a carrier bag and pick up any likely-looking pebbles.
When you have a few, line them all up and take a second look. Once you
have a number of pebbles together it's easy to see which ones really look
like hearts and which don't. Just pick one. After a while you will start
to spot these in other places too – for example, in the soil in your own
garden, or maybe on a walk to a local wood or forest. Even one heart-
shaped pebble is pretty. Lean it against a plant pot so that it can easily
be seen.

Pots in my garden are decorated with angel plant sticks, and with angels that sit on the side of the pots. If you're craft-minded, why not stencil angels onto the side of the pots in your garden? Try working with just one colour (maybe silver, gold or cream) for a more sophisticated look. Use suitable outdoor paints or varnish to protect your artwork.

When my daughters were young we used to collect and paint pebbles from the garden. Why not have a go at this yourself? You can use indelible pens or paint and then varnish your stones. Write letters on each pebble to spell out words ('safe', 'protected', 'angels', 'peace', and so on) or inscribe magical symbols. The children used to paint butterflies and ladybirds.

You can create a grotto-type effect using an existing water feature as the centrepiece. Decorate a wall area with crystals, shells and pretty stones, using plaster or cement. Leave spaces to add tea-lights, or add hooks to the wall from which to hang lanterns, to create garden spaces suitable for relaxation and dining.

I have an altar tree in my garden – well, to be fair, it's actually a tree stump. The original tree was cut down by the previous owners and they added wire around the stump to support climbing, scented plants so that they could smother it with colour. I've enhanced the whole thing by tying hair ribbons at various places. It's a variation on an ancient theme of making a wishing tree (more on this later, see page 73).

Angel garden house

If you live in an area where it's too cold to enjoy outdoor space most of the year, how about creating an 'angel house' in your garden? First of all you'll need a small shed. If you already have one that you can reassign, so much the better. If not, find out when your local supplier has a sale; look in your local shop at the postcard ads; or search recycling websites for your area. Pick a shed with windows. Decorate it by painting it with garden-fence stain (pink, lilac or pale blue), add pieces of decorative edging to the underside of the roof and put a pretty sign on the door.

If you have an old piece of carpet that you can place on the floor, even better. You could also insulate the inside by adding an extra layer of wood or board. Your special hideout is a great place to meditate or watch the birds through the window: place your bird feeders right outside. If it's cold, take a hot-water bottle with you and use battery-operated lamps. Never take a flame of any sort into your wooden shed, but I think that goes without saying! Over the last couple of years I've seen flickering, battery-operated candles: these would be wonderful, as you'd get the same ambience, without the danger of a live flame.

If you live in a part of the world where you get plenty of sunshine, you will get even more use from your 'angel house'. Make sure it's kept regularly dusted and swept, to keep spiders at bay. You could pile cushions inside, read books here, and even create a special garden or path leading to your magical space. Place a few slabs, bricks or pebbles to create the path; then place mini wooden edging on either side, or line the path with pots of herbs or scented flowers. How about placing an archway in the garden, which you have to walk under to reach your new space? You could even add a little gateway (painted pretty colours, of course). If you are close to an outdoor electrical socket, you could add some lantern-type coloured lights around the roof (ensure they are the outdoor sort, not the kind that you add to an indoor tree).

If you have a bigger shed, you could include wicker-type garden furniture piled high with cushions (bring the chairs in when it's cold so that they don't get damp). Imagine snuggling up in a chair with the doors wide open on a summer's day. How about making some simple curtains? Using an end of fabric, hem around the edges (no need to line them), then make a wider fold along the top edge and thread some net-curtain wire through it. Suspend the curtain at your windows using hooks. I tie mine back with pieces of coloured ribbon – gorgeous!

Angel-wish tree

As I mentioned earlier, I have an old tree stump in my garden that I decorate with ribbons. The stump is tall and has a certain something about it – I always felt it needed some respect. It is wrapped in lengths of wire to support climbing and scented plants, and I tied a selection of coloured ribbons to the wire and to the stump itself.

The ribbons are given to the tree as a sort of offering – I connect to my angels when I tie the ribbons on. My ribbons are mainly the ties sewn inside clothes by manufacturers, to help the clothes hang better in the shop. I always snip them out once I've got the items home, so this is a great way of recycling (I'm big on that, as you can tell). Each time I add a new ribbon I bless the tree and request a 'favour' from the angels (or, traditionally, from the faeries or the tree itself). I'm not sure if it works or not, but for me it's just a bit of fun, and it sure looks pretty. Why not give it a go?

This is a variation on an old theme. Angel-wish trees were generally selected because of a unique or special appearance. Offerings were then made to the tree (scraps of cloth, coins, shells or pretty pebbles, for example), in exchange for a wish. It's a little like the ancient practice of throwing a coin into a wishing well. Sometimes the offering was made in exchange for 'safe passage' – the ancient Romans would always offer a coin before they crossed over water.

Similar tree decorations can still be found around the world next to the sites of old wells. Strips of cloth are tied to the tree, with requests for healing and help written on them. Sometimes people miss the point, though, and trees next to old water sources near my home in Cornwall can be covered in all sorts of rubbish – I've seen scraps of paper, a luggage label and once even a pair of old socks! I've also seen flags and objects made of twigs, twine and cereal crops, as well as baby bibs, ties, wool and photographs pegged to the branches. If you do this at a traditional site, be respectful – your rubbish has to be cleared by somebody. Below are a few suggestions that you might like to consider.

Coins

Occasionally you'll find a tree with coins pressed into the bark. This is thought of as a lucky tree, and the coins are an offering, and in exchange the tree is meant to bring you good luck (hopefully in the form of money!). It's exciting to take part in this ritual, and if you ever find a tree with coins in it, I guarantee you'll be searching around for a coin of your own – a shoe makes a great 'away-from-home' hammer with which to press your coin into the bark. Be careful, though; don't remove coins from a money tree, as it's said to anger the pixies – you have been warned!

Crystals

Tina, a dear old friend of mine (no longer on this side of life), had a beautiful old tree at the front of her property. A small natural hole in the trunk was the perfect place to add a crystal, and over time the tree claimed the precious stone and grew around it completely. I thought it was the most wonderful offering.

Other natural ideas

If you have a suitable tree in your own garden, maybe you'd like to continue some of these magical rituals. But if you don't have a wishing tree or an outdoor space, you can always do your rituals in a park or wood. Remember not to litter (and that includes ribbon-tying), but you could leave natural offerings such as carved pieces of unvarnished and

untreated wood (not something too precious, though, for remember that any items you leave may be removed by others), shells, nuts and seeds or pretty stones. You can also use garden twine, which is made of natural materials and will eventually rot away.

Stone-lore

How about offering special stones at your sacred site? Look out for heart-shaped pebbles (see page 70) and stones with holes in them. Stones with natural holes are considered magical. You are most likely to find these next to the sea, in a stream or riverbed or on the shores of a lake or pond. Line up small pebbles around a tree (not heavy stones, which might be dangerous for others if they topple over).

Holes were often cut into stones in the ancient world. It's believed such stones were used for ritualistic purposes, and some holes were even big enough to climb through. The rituals varied, but in some rites stones were climbed through to promote healing and protection, while in other rituals one stepped through a stone hole or slit to enter another world or dimension.

You can also create a circle of stones or pebbles on your own ground. Such stone circles have been used for centuries, and large sites of standing stone circles have been discovered all over the world, their original purpose long since obscured, although they are thought to have been used as places of ritual, burial sites or meeting places, or to mark the changes of the seasons using astrology.

Small pebble circles were created by Native Americans and were called medicine wheels. They were used as sacred circles and were often divided into four parts or quarters. To create your own medicine wheel, use similar-sized pebbles with a larger stone at each corner to represent north, south, east and west (use a compass to get the directions correct). Mark a cross of stones through the centre, taking your row of stones diagonally from the large 'directional stones'. You might wish to add a larger stone or even a crystal at your centre point. If you wish, you can also include other natural objects as part of your arrangement.

I sometimes use a selection of tumbled (smooth-edged) crystals to create a temporary medicine wheel on my desk. It's a ritual that is very relaxing, and a useful distraction if I need a break from my work!

The centre of the medicine wheel represents the Creator, or the place where the visible and invisible realms meet. It's fun to incorporate these magical rituals into your life. Look out for magnetic hematite, a shiny black stone. You can occasionally buy this in strips of magnetized stones, which attract each other and snap together. I guarantee you'll play with them for hours!

You can create a more permanent circle in your garden by setting stones, pebbles and slate or terracotta pieces into sand. Lay down an area of sand about 10–15 cm (4–6 in) deep. Mark a circle in the sand, then press in a round of similar-sized and similar-coloured pebbles; then make another circle using a different shape and colour. Continue in decreasing circles until you come to the middle. Perhaps you could add something really special to the centre, like a piece of crystal (for larger pieces of rose quartz and amethyst, visit your local tropical-fish shop).

How can you bring a little angel magic into your own home or garden? What can you recycle, make or find on nature walks? Your displays can be ever-changing with the seasons or to suit specific occasions. Just go and have some fun!

We love to work with you on creative endeavours. Ask us, your angels, to inspire you in your artwork.

Angels and children

We watch over your children
as if they were our own

Angels have always taken care of children, and there are many ancient stories about this. Do you have such stories from when you were younger? Do you recall times when unexplained phenomena occurred? Maybe you sensed or felt something around you that was not of this realm.

As we have seen, angels help with healing and protection, and many people have shared their stories of angel intervention at times of difficulty when they were young. During illness and operations, when children are confined to bed in hospital, many youngsters talk about the 'lady' who sits by the bed – the one no one else can see! It's during such times of health crisis that deceased loved ones also appear. Our little ones are loved by the angels in exactly the same way they would be if the children were their very own. Our innocent little ones are cared for by guardians on both sides of life.

True-life story
Healing angels

Last year I asked for healing and help from the angels to help my friend's son, who was taken into the Special Baby Unit straight after he was born. Scans and various other tests were done and they thought he might have been born with meningitis. When the tests came back everything was clear, he started feeding properly and he hasn't looked back since. He is now a very cheeky, adorable one-year-old, who is definitely an 'old soul'.

How angels can help troubled children

Anxious children will often settle better after discussions about guardian angels and their roles in our lives. Have you spoken to your children about angels yet? You can easily purchase teddy bears with angel wings, storybooks about our magical friends and other items for their bedrooms. Maybe you could create a pair of cream satin wings to attach to a child's much-loved stuffed toy.

How about doing a visualization with your child so that they can 'imagine' what their own angel might look like? Let's have a go.

Exercise
Children's angel meditation for bedtime

Follow your usual routine, but, instead of a bedtime story, read out the following meditation for your child. Make the lighting in the room dim (use a low-energy bulb or a plug-in night-light, and if you wish you can also play a relaxing music track in the background (use something without words, an unhurried 'angelic track'). Read through the following meditation a couple of times so that you can practise doing it at a really leisurely pace.

Eventually you won't need to read the meditation; you can simply play the music (vary it from time to time) and your child will be able to 'meet their angel' on their own. Read very, very slowly and quietly. The sound of your voice will help to relax your child into a deep and peaceful sleep. Before you do this you can ask your child if their guardian angel is a 'he' or a 'she' (trust me, they will tell you!), and then make sure you use male or female in the correct place here.

1 Close your eyes, darling ... it's nice and safe – everything is okay. We're going to go on a special journey to meet your guardian angel ... Relax ... Your angel is your invisible guardian who looks after you and takes care of you every day, and every night ... Relax ... Just relax and snuggle down in your warm and comfortable bed.

2 Take a deep breath in through your nose ... Hold the breath for just a second, and then blow it out again like this [make a long, slow blowing sound here] ... And again ... Breathe in ... hold it, hold it, and then breathe out again like this [make a blowing sound]. Now breathe normally: in ... and out ... in ... [read slowly] and out ... just like the waves at the seaside ... In ... and out ... like waves crashing on the shore ... in ... and out ... Relax ... relax ...

3 Imagine you are floating – floating gently just like a leaf in the breeze ... floating ... floating ... safe and secure ... nice and relaxed ... Floating gently now, just like a butterfly ... flying around the garden ... flittering up through the trees ... sometimes landing on a flower ... Relax now ... just relax ...

4 Your beautiful guardian angel is here [add child's name] … standing next to Mummy (Daddy, Auntie, and so on) … We can't see him (or her) with our eyes, but we can see him (her) in our head … Just relax … Your angel has fluffy wings like a baby chick … Your angel is surrounded by a pretty white light … He (she) is glowing and twinkling … he's (she's) a magical angel and his (her) job is to look after you and help keep you safe …

5 Your angel has a big happy smile … We love angels, and angels love us – they are our friends … Your angel surrounds us with a big angel hug … Can you feel the love from the angel? [whisper] Can you feel your angel's wings wrapped around you? Just float on by now … just like that butterfly … up and up, up and up …

6 Our angels help us to feel safe and take care of us when we are frightened or worried. Your guardian angel is always with you, keeping you safe … looking after you … Just float now … just relax … float nice and gently.

7 Your angel is sending a magical tingling feeling through your body ... This is special angel protection ... If you lie still you will feel it now [keep quiet for a moment here] ... Feel the wonderful tingling feeling ... [keep quiet for a moment here].

8 Your angel is so special, and his (her) only job is to take care of you ... Whenever you need him (her), just ask him (her) to come and stand behind you ... He (she) will be wearing an invisible cloak, but you will still know he (she) is there ... Just relax ... everything is peaceful and calm ... you are safe ... Your glowing white and sparkling angel is always with you.

9 Do you want to ask your angel a question? You can ask anything you like ... [suggest something here – pick different questions each time; below are a few]
• Let's ask your guardian angel his (her) name.
• Let's ask your angel to look after you at school.
• Let's ask your angel to be with you when you ride your bike.
[Give your child a little time to do this; don't speak for two or three minutes.]

10 Now it's time to go to sleep ... Your angel will stay here all night to make sure you have a lovely sleep and nice dreams ... Your angel will go on your dream adventures with you ... Good night, angel [if your child suggests a name for the angel, make sure you use that name here].

11 Let's do this now ... drift gently off to sleep. Relax ... floating nice and gently ... Relax ... [whispering now] Relax ... relax ... [even quieter] Relax ... relax ...

Now back quietly out of the room. It can be useful to have a dimmer switch in a child's bedroom so that you can slowly dim the lights during the meditation.

If you have time the following morning, ask your child about their dreams and how they slept. You might be surprised.

Angels at bedtime

It's a clever idea to frame an angel picture and hang it in your child's bedroom (maybe at the foot of the bed, so that your child can see it when in bed). Take photographs together of angels in churches and old buildings, and let your child choose an image, or order a poster to frame from a specialist supplier on the internet.

Older children might like to draw their own angel. After a few meditation sessions perhaps they will have a clear image of what their angel looks like. Make pieces of art: use glitter, tinsel and shiny paper for the wings. If you're really serious, you can find 'wing' templates on the internet; or use bird wings as a guide.

Let the child choose their favourite image and have it framed. You could cut out angel faces and get your child to create the angel's gowns using paper doilies (available from supermarkets, cake shops and art shops): white, gold and silver circles of shiny paper with cut-out lacy patterns on them. Don't forget to write the angel's name on the picture too (let the child choose their angel's name, or ask for a name during their angel meditation).

Angels and babies

Have you ever seen a newborn baby suddenly stop feeding and look up into the air, giggling? Don't you know they can see angels? My eight-month-old granddaughter laughs happily at something – or someone – that the rest of us cannot see! And one of my own daughters, aged nearly two, pointed to the ceiling many years ago and said, excitedly, 'Look, Mummy, a faerie man!'

When your youngsters are old enough to speak, ask them what they see (make a note for the child; record all their experiences in a special notebook, so that they have the memories to look back on (not every child will recall the experiences they had with the angels). And ask your little one's angels to watch over them whilst they sleep.

True-life story

An angel to watch over you

My ten-year-old son was worried one evening when we told him we were moving to a new house and he would have to go to a new school. He went up to bed quite upset.

During the early hours of the morning he came through to our bedroom and seemed really startled and shaken. When I asked him what the matter was, he said he had seen a lady dressed in a white gown, with her hands clasped together as if she was praying; he said she was glowing. The lady stood in his doorway for a few seconds, looking at him, as though to reassure him; and then she disappeared.

I believe that she was an angel visiting my son to reassure him at his time of worry.

Angelic protection for children with worries

Like the little boy in the true-life story earlier, children have many worries; and, as with adults, it doesn't matter how small the problem is, the issue is important to the child. Talking about how angels walk beside them, or telling them stories about other children who've had real-life encounters with them, really helps to establish a strong rapport with angels in general. Remind your child to 'ask their angels' in every situation and, as they learn from examples, let them see you use this technique too:

- Ask the angels to help you find parking spaces – when you forget, your child will begin to remind you!
- Ask the angels to assist you when you lose something. It's amazing how often those missing car keys will turn up just after you've asked for help. Again, next time something is missing, your child will probably remind you: 'Ask the angels.'
- When you are short of cash and in need of a particular item, ask the angels to help bring it into your life cheaply or for free. Tell others you've done this, and let your child help so that they can see how positive thinking/creative visualization works.
- When children see you request angelic assistance, they will naturally begin to work with angels in their own lives.

True-life story

Protected by angels

My son Josh, who has just turned six, often talks to his angels, especially when he is unwell (he suffers terribly from food allergies and asthma). A couple of weeks ago I'd taken him to the beach and, when he lost sight of me for a moment, he thought he was lost. This wasn't the case because I could see him, but he couldn't see me. As I watched him panic, he suddenly calmed down, turned in my direction and walked in a straight line towards me. I asked him why he was upset and he explained that he'd lost sight of me, but had asked his 'kind lady' to help. He explained that 'his lady' took him by the hand and brought him to me. Now at no point did I see a lady with him, but later that day I found a tiny white feather in his pocket!

When I ask him about his angels, sometimes he will tell me everything and at other times he can be quite cagey about it all. I find it a great comfort, though. One day my son told me that the angels had taken Granddad. I noted the time, and it turned out that it was the precise time when Granddad had actually passed away. My son is my little angel!

Colouring

I did a search on the internet and found numerous black-and-white angel images that were perfect for colouring. Some are even labelled as children's colouring pages. If you are good with a computer, then you can search for these and print a few off; if not, ask someone else to do it for you.

If you're good at sketching, why not draw angel outlines using a black felt-tip pen for your child to colour in? Trace them from Christmas cards, or look for stencil shapes from craft shops. Children can have hours of 'old-fashioned' fun with a few colouring sheets, some coloured pencils or felt-tip pens (washable ones, of course!).

Let's play dressing-up

Are you clever with a sewing machine? If not, maybe another relative is. Dressing-up is something you can do together on a wet afternoon at home. Save frilly nightdresses and pretty petticoats to make angel gowns. Or, if you prefer, you can buy angel outfits quite cheaply (my local supermarket often has them, or try party shops or the internet). Make sure all items are age-appropriate (wands and crowns are often made of sharp plastic).

Here are a few suggestions for angel items:

- Try an old wooden spoon wrapped in tin foil as a wand (also useful for budding faeries). Stick a silver star on it, or curl some tinsel around the top.
- Need a magical crown or halo? Cut a strip of card from an old cereal box (about 6 cm (2¾ in) wide and 4 cm (1½ in) longer than the width of your child's head). Wrap it in tin foil and then staple it together in a band (the size of your child's head). If you don't mind the mess, help your child to attach jewels or glitter.
- Want an angel skirt? Thread some wide elastic through the top of a strip of net curtain. Tie together, then trim the bottom to the right length (no need to hem or join it together).

Cooking

How about making up a batch of cupcakes with your child (see page 90)? You can use a packet mix if you prefer, and bake your cakes in pretty paper wrappers. Once they are out of the oven and cool, decorate them with icing and 'angel dust' (edible cake glitter). Keep an eye out for suitable cake decorations when you're out shopping. Decorations usually have a long shelf life, so you can keep them in stock for when you need them. Butterflies, birds and flowers are all in keeping with the theme.

You can even make a cake with angel wings. Cut a slice off the top of the cake, divide it in half and then put a blob of butter icing in the middle of the top of the cake. 'Glue' the halves back onto the cake with the icing; place the rounded part of the slice into the icing and point the widest part out and upwards to make 'angel wings'. Great fun for kids … and don't forget to wear aprons!

Exercise

Magical angel cupcakes

These cupcakes are really easy to make and only need a few simple ingredients. If you prefer, you can buy a packet mix from your local supermarket and just follow the instructions.

Makes 12 small cakes

100 g (4 oz) softened butter
100 g (4 oz) caster sugar
2 large eggs, beaten
100 g (4 oz) self-raising flour
1 level teaspoon baking powder
Selection of icing and toppings, to decorate

1 Preheat the oven to 190°C/375°F/gas mark 5.

2 Pop 12 paper cases into the holes of a 12-section muffin tin.

3 Beat the butter and sugar together, using a wooden spoon or hand mixer, until the mixture goes pale and fluffy.

4 Add the beaten egg, mixing in a little at a time.

5 Sift in half of the flour and fold gently into the mixture. Then mix in the other half and the baking powder.

6 Divide the mixture between the paper cases, and bake for 12 minutes or until risen and golden on top. Allow to cool for 10 minutes on a rack, before removing from the tin.

7 When cool, top with butter icing (softened butter and icing sugar mixed together), or bought frosting/icing mixture.

8 Decorate with cherries, nuts, icing 'jewels', cake jellies, sugar strands (hundred and thousands) and so on.

Angel blessing

Angels love to take care of our human babies and children. It is perfectly acceptable to ask them to take care of your little ones. Don't worry if you forget – know that the angels are with your children at all times.

Psychic children

One trend in my postbag that doesn't seem to have gone away is parents writing in about their psychic children. I've written previously about the numerous children around the world who seem to be born with extraordinary talents and psychic abilities. I even wrote a book about the subject. Some of the children appear to be in higher contact with the angelic realms or tell us they work directly with God. There seems no reason to doubt them. Their talents include:

* Telepathy (mind-reading and mind-communication)
* Healing
* Spirit contact (seeing and hearing angels and the souls of deceased humans, and having the ability to communicate with them)
* The ability to see into the future (telling their female relatives they are pregnant, for example, and even knowing the sex of the child)

The list goes on and on, and I suspect that psychic children are advanced souls who are incarnating with other etheric beings (angels, for example) at this time of great change on Earth. Let's face it, we need all the assistance we can get, as we've certainly messed things up in the last few decades. Since the start of the Industrial Revolution we've scarred the Earth and polluted it. Are they here to help with these things?

The children say yes. Some are in regular contact with their 'home planets' (I know this sounds completely bizarre, but bear with me) and bring words of wisdom to their parents. They also pass on information about the Earth and humankind that is well beyond their years.

True-life story

Working with the angels

Tyler has always been spiritually attuned, and one day he asked me if I knew the name of his angel. I tuned in and said her name was Olithia. He wanted to see her. So I sat down with him and guided him through a meditation. When he came back, he saw exactly the scene and image that I had seen. He was amazed and adored her from that moment. Olithia is now as much a part of his life as we are. He cannot talk to his dad about her, as his father does not believe. But he talks to me and my partner, and I love the fact that she has helped him through so much. My son even told me, from the age of just two, that angels made him. He used to point and say 'Angel'.

Some people may say that my children are influenced by me being a medium. However, until they started showing an interest I didn't speak to them about it, as I did not want them to say things at school that might single them out. Angels are a very open thing for us now. We sing to the angels and call them in when we want to feel really happy, or nice and calm. I would not have it any other way.

Encouraging children to work with angels

How can you interact with the children in your life to encourage them to work with angels? Angels can be a supportive source in children's lives, and many younger children (as we've seen from the stories in this chapter) can even see their angels. Have a play with some of the ideas in this chapter, and maybe you and your child can come up with some fun ideas of your own.

Children, ask us to support and protect you. Know that we always love you without question.

Furry and feathered angel friends

We help you in many ways, sometimes appearing to you as creatures of the Earth

Animals on Earth are God's gift to humankind. All around the world new creatures are being discovered each year, many in the depths of the rainforests or at the bottom of the deepest oceans. With today's technology we can admire everything from the most exotic of birds to the humblest field mouse. Images are beamed right into our living rooms, as brave camera-crews fly all around the world bringing visual specimens into our homes. It makes it easy to remember how magical our world really is.

Some animals live a little closer to home, though, and our favourites are the animals we choose to live with in our homes. You may be familiar with dogs, cats, rabbits and so on, but the types of pets that we choose as companions vary dramatically around the world. Monkeys and even skunks are common pets in some places. But the reasons why we choose to share our homes with pets is much the same worldwide, and companionship is right up there at the top of the list. Our pets are literally our guardian angels, and my books are full of stories of animals caring for their human owners and of pets even saving their lives.

Angel blessing

Create a special notebook full of memories of your beloved pets – one book for each animal. Draw sketches, take photographs and write down memories of your time together as they happen. Recall why you are thankful that your furry angel is in your life. These books make beautiful mementos for the future, and I know you'll love looking back on them.

Angel dog to the rescue

These days science is beginning to understand the intelligence of what we once thought of as 'dumb' animals. Animals don't think in the way that humans do, but they are clever in their own way. Dogs in particular have been trained to sniff out drugs and other contraband at airports; they are also used as 'eyes' for the visually impaired. We've discovered that some dogs can smell cancer in humans, and can even be trained

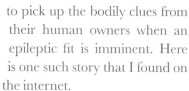

to pick up the bodily clues from their human owners when an epileptic fit is imminent. Here is one such story that I found on the internet.

Edward, a Golden Retriever, is officially recognized as the carer of a lady in Devon – he actually gets paid for his help! The carer's allowance helps to pay for his food and toys. Wendy suffers from a skin condition with several complications. Her dog Edward has been taught to do all sorts of jobs around the house, including emptying the washing machine. He has also saved Wendy's life on numerous occasions after she's stopped breathing in while bed at night. The clever dog wakes his owner's husband to alert him to the danger.

When we're lonely or sad, angels often bring us companions. Sometimes those companions may be of the furry or feathered kind. Pets often provide the love and loyalty that may be missing from our lives – our very own angels on Earth.

Angel blessing

It really is a blessing to have pets in your life. The opportunity to care for God's creatures brings us so much pleasure in return. Remember to thank your angels for helping to bring your furry and feathered friends into your life, and thank your pet for sharing his or her life with you. On some higher level of consciousness, your pet will definitely get the message.

Fun ways to bring angels into your pet's life

I remember that we once owned a pair of feather 'angel wings', which we'd purchased to hang on our Christmas tree at home. Our rescue dog, Lady, was a very small breed, and one of the children placed the elastic from the wings around the dog's waist just long enough to take a photograph. She was very placid and didn't mind one bit (animals are often very tolerant of their owners' whims). The wings stuck out behind her and she looked just like an angel-dog! Sadly it was only a few months later that she passed away, but we always have that memory of her, and now she is an angel for real.

Pets have angels too. Why not paint or sew a little 'Protected by angels' sign to hang on your pet's bedding? I was doing some research on the internet for a magazine column once and came across pet tags

that were pressed into the shape of cats and dogs with wings on. The tags were for inscribing the pet's name and the owner's telephone number, and clipped onto the pet's collar just like normal tags. I loved the idea and included it in my angel column. Several manufacturers have now created 'angel tags' for pets. Next time your pet needs a new tag, ask for these at your specialist pet shop, or simply do a search on the internet.

Many years ago I lost two of my cats on the same day. After weeks of searching and asking around, they never turned up. I always like to think that someone took a fancy to them and took them home. It was comforting to me to imagine that they were being looked after somewhere else. I was lucky enough to have a great photograph of the two of them cuddling up together on a chair. All these years later I am able to accept that they have probably passed away. The photograph is very precious to me, and I keep it on a windowsill in a special angel-decorated frame. Maybe you could do the same with photos of your own pets, both living and passed-over ones. The important thing is to take the photograph in the first place. Many people never think to do this. So take a photo of your own pet today.

Ariel, archangel of animals

The archangels are known as ministering angels. These great beings have vast roles, and animals have their very own archangel taking care of them and watching over them. The Archangel Ariel fulfils this special role; he's pretty well in charge of the natural world and also watches over the nature beings (faeries). His name means 'lion of God' and this is meant

to be reflected in his appearance, although some believe that Ariel is a feminine energy. When this archangel is around you, you'll encounter many images of lions or references to them. Here is a list of Ariel's general roles:

• Agriculture
• Animal breeding
• Animal control/care
• Birds
• Conservation
• Fishing
• Forestry
• Game
• Sciences that relate to the Earth, marine areas,
  space, nuclear energy
• Tree surgery
• Veterinary work
• Water treatment
• Wildlife

Ariel takes care of animals of the Earth (including pets), birds and fish. Here is a little more about him and his associations. If you want to bring in colours, crystals or oils associated with this angel, for your angel displays or altars, use the table opposite for reference.

True-life story
Just a little while more ...

My lovely dog Roly, a Lhasa Apso, was just seven years old. He had a problem with his brain and we came to the difficult decision to have him put to sleep the next day.

As you can imagine, we were really upset, but decided to take him on one last evening walk. Suddenly Roly ran off and went right up to the edge of the main road. We rushed over to him – we didn't want him to die in a car accident or hurt anyone else if he ran into the road. But the dog had alerted us to a drunken man who was lying on the edge of the kerb having

Archangel Ariel's associations

Item	Association with Ariel
Candle colours	Sky-blue and gold for your rituals and angel altar
Crystals	Rose-quartz, moonstone, pink tourmaline, amethyst, sugulite, emerald, jade
Chakra	Third-eye chakra, the part of the emotional body (aura body) at the point between the eyes
Element	Earth (and sometimes air)
Trees and plants	Birch, ivy, sage
Patron	Of animals, fish and birds
Essential oils	Cardamom, rose, sandalwood, yarrow
Earth-element oils	Patchouli, coriander, sandalwood, ginger, cedarwood

You can use any of these things in your angel work. Meditate on questions relating to your animals by holding one of the crystals listed above and burning a sky-blue or gold candle, for example. See if you feel inspired to create rituals of your own. There is no right or wrong way to do them as long as: you harm no one and nothing when you create your ritual; you hold positive and loving thoughts in your mind as you do it; you do the ritual for positive and loving reasons (in the same way that you might perform a spell); and your intent is high, moral and legal.

a heart attack! My husband and I managed to pull him to safety and called the emergency services. Our dog literally saved the man's life, and after that we felt our pet was an earth angel.

Because of saving the man, we decided not to have Roly put to sleep the next day. He'd saved a human life, so we thought we'd do everything we could for him too. Roly lived for another year, and we gave him the best life we could. Sadly he did get worse eventually and, after another hard decision and following the vet's advice, he was finally put to sleep.

We never regretted giving him that extra year of life, and he did return in spirit about a month later. I felt him sit by my side for a couple of minutes, and then I sensed that he said goodbye and ran off outside across the patio. I knew then that Roly was back to his normal self, and it was such a comfort. I felt him in the garden a couple of times later on, and then he never returned. I knew he had gone back to his heavenly home and I was happy for him.

Angel altar/display for your pets

There are suggestions for angel altars and displays throughout the book, but this one is especially for your pets. If possible, collect together some framed photographs of your pets, both living and passed over. If you don't have photographs of your pet, you can use something else to represent your pet, such as an animal figurine, a photo that reminds you of a special pose your pet might have taken or a picture of a similar breed. On a table, a shelf or the corner of a cupboard, lay down some sort of display cloth (a scarf, napkin, tablecloth, and so on), then create your animal altar:

- Add the photographs or representations of your pet.
- Include an angel figurine – in pride of place, right at the centre back of your display. Some gift shops/internet stores sell angel figurines holding animals (cats, dogs) or standing alongside bigger animals (horses). If you're craft-minded, try making your own figurine with air-drying clay.
- Add something that represents Ariel's association with the element of earth. I use a bowl of sand with a selection of crystals. If deep enough, the sand can also hold an incense stick and safely catch the ash from it (change it frequently to keep it fresh).

- Add a scented candle if you wish, using the oils listed in the table. If you find these difficult to obtain, put a few drops of aromatherapy oil in your aromatherapy burner (following the manufacturer's instructions).
- Keep your angel books, angel cards and other angel products alongside your display, and sit next to it when you pray (to your Creator) or meditate. You can also arrange your display on a table close to where you read or relax.
- Add fresh flowers to energize the display, and ask the angels to watch over your pets on both sides of life.
- Create a special mantra (a positive saying that you can repeat each time you pass your display). It can be something simple like: 'Angels, please take care of my pet, thank you.'
- If you own a pack of angel cards, there might be one that is suitable for your display – prop it up in a prominent place.
- Once you get used to seeing the display and it no longer excites you, it's time to change the cloth and flowers and rearrange everything; or add or remove some items. Keep the arrangement around as long as it uplifts you. When you're bored with it, do it again!

Afterlife contact

You can use your animal display as a point of focus for making contact with the energy of a pet that has passed over. Using the photo on the display, think back to a happy time that you spent together. If you feel a little emotional, that's okay – it just means you are making a loving connection. In your mind, thank your pet for the time you spent together and wish it lots of love and comfort in its new heavenly home.

If you wish, you can also ask your pet's heavenly guardian (their angel or animal guide) to bring your pet forward in a dream-visitation, to let you know it is safe and well. This would probably only happen once, because naturally it's important that we move on in our earthly lives. Over the years people have shared all sorts of experiences with me. Here are a few:

- A hamster appeared in a dream.
- A horse was there to meet its owner during a near-death experience.
- Dogs have rubbed up against their owners' legs or been heard barking.

- Cats have jumped up on the bed when their owners are sleeping (you may even see an indentation in the quilt where they have lain down next to you in their spirit bodies).
- A family pig was heard making its usual snuffling sound – both owners jumped up and noticed the familiar noise at the same time.

After my own dog, Lady, passed on, she appeared to me in a dream-visitation experience. She looked younger and healthier than when she passed over, and bounced around like a puppy. Lady had also brought a whole stack of dogs with her – dogs I'd grown up with. Strangely, the only one that was missing was an annoying Jack Russell that had bitten and scarred my lip when I was a little girl. Perhaps Lady felt I wouldn't appreciate a visit from a dog that had hurt me!

True-life story
New friend appears in a dream

My darling Lurcher, Larry, appeared to me in a dream after he died. I was so pleased to see him. He walked into my bedroom and had another dog with him; it was another black Lurcher, just like Larry. I didn't recognize the dog, but it was sweet and put its paws up onto the bed. Six months later we found a black Lurcher that had been rescued from a kennel in Ireland and she is now part of our family. We've called her Lily. I really believe Larry was introducing us to our future pet and giving permission for her to live with us. We were so worried about what he might think about being replaced, but the dream really reassured us.

Angel healing for pets

When your pet is sick or you are worried about it for any reason, just call upon the Archangel Ariel to help. This treatment is a complementary therapy and works alongside care given by your vet. Always seek professional medical treatment if your pet is unwell.

1 Imagine Ariel beaming down rays of healing light upon your pet.

2 Hold your hands over your animal and ask that Ariel helps you make it well. Imagine those healing rays pouring down through your body and out through your hands. As you do so, you will feel more relaxed and healed yourself, as you take on the positive effects of the healing.

3 Imagine any illness draining out of your pet and being absorbed into the ground, ready to be neutralized by the earth.

4 You can also place suitable crystals (see the table on page 46) around or on your pet, if it is safe and appropriate to do so (please ensure that the crystals do not become a swallowing hazard for young children).

True-life story
Angel healing stranger

My little dog Troy had been very poorly with epilepsy and seemed to be going rapidly downhill. He was very wobbly, trembling and having regular fits. Then yesterday I took him out for a walk. He really wasn't well enough, and I ended up having to carry him – I thought it would be worth it and just give him a little boost being outside. Whilst we were out we met a very nice elderly man. He explained to me that he was a healer. He put his hands on Troy, and five minutes later my boy was bouncing around like a puppy. He's had another good day again today. I think the stranger really was an angel in human form.

True-life story
Spiritual healing

I work a lot with the Archangel Michael, and I really feel he helped me with my dog. My Dachshund was very poorly; the vet said it was a slipped disc in her spine, and wanted £2,500 to operate there and then. I decided to start her off with spiritual healing for just ten minutes a day, calling on the Archangel Michael to help me. It worked and she's still going strong.

Safe on the Other Side

Sometimes, when a pet's natural end-of-life has been reached, you can ask the angels to come and collect your pet and take it safely to the Other Side. You can be secure in the knowledge that it is being taken care of by special animal carers in the afterlife. It is possible for passed-over pets to be looked after by deceased family members and friends in the afterlife, and I've written about many cases where deceased loved ones visit in dreamlike visitations, bringing the pets with them. This can be wonderfully comforting for everyone concerned. Such experiences always feel more real than normal dreams, indicating the difference between a dream and a visitation – our bodies are still asleep, but during dream-visitation experiences our minds are lucid and aware.

My late father often brings a whole assortment of pets with him – some I remember, and others I have no memory of at all. I guess they must be animals that were important to him in his life on Earth. It's so lovely that they are all together now.

Our special pets are angels on earth. Remember to tell your pet today just how much they mean to you, and ask the angels to watch over them every single day.

True-life story
New cat for old

I had a ginger cat, which unfortunately got run over several years ago. A few days after it happened, I saw him asleep at the end of my bed where he usually lay. I could hear him purring. Then I had a dream in which I saw a black and white cat lying on my bed.

A couple of days later I told a work colleague about losing my cat. She later said that she had a relative who needed to rehome a black and white kitten – was I interested? I said yes, and a few days later this kitten arrived. I had not intended to get another cat so soon, but I think my ginger cat thought otherwise. My new cat lies in the same spot on my bed.

In loving memory

We are truly blessed to have our pets in our lives, but once they pass over it's often hard to grieve in the way that we'd like to. Make full use of any photographs that you have of your pet, perhaps collecting your memories together in an album; or build a memorial website dedicated to your pet. Don't forget to include pictures of angels, to remind yourself that your special friend is being taken care of in his or her new home.

True-life stories
Happy in Heaven

My darling Spaniel of 16 years appeared to me in a dream. She was running and bouncing through the clouds, like she used to in the fields on our walks at home, when she was younger. She looked so happy that I woke up crying.

The animals on Earth are as important to us as our human friends. Know that we take care of your pets as we do of your children.

Living with the angels

We are with you, supporting you every single day

Are angels a part of your everyday life? They can be! Angels are with us, but we can choose to include them in everything we do. Talk to them, listen to them, ask them for advice. Make them a part of your life by choice. Of course there are many different types of angels – as many angels as you could need – and plenty to go around. Whatever help you require, there will be an angel that can help you. Here are just a few of them.

Angels of love

Angels offer us the sort of unconditional love that you have probably never experienced. During my workshops I often take students through a 'meet your guardian angel' guided meditation. When I get to the part where my students receive unconditional love from their angel, many people cry. We're just not used to being loved for no reason at all. It brings on great remembrance – a knowing that we've had this sort of love previously (from our Creator God) and will one day experience it again. (I have created a meditation CD for people who are unable to attend my workshops; try asking at your local library for it.) Remember the angel's unconditional love every time you need a little reassurance.

Exercise
Angel-hug experience

Do you need a little love and comfort and have no one around to give you this? Why not ask your angels to give you a loving hug?

1 Find a comfortable chair to snuggle up in, then wrap yourself in a blanket (if you feel cold) and close your eyes.

2 Imagine your guardian angel is standing right behind you. Feel the loving energy pulsing from your angel into and right around your body. Feel the sensation of pure, unconditional love … Relax and expect to feel the love – just let it happen.

3 Feel your angel wrap his angel wings around your whole body in a giant angel-hug. Just relax into the hug. There are no expectations from you – nothing is needed except that you enjoy the experience and feel healed by it. Let this go on for as long as you need it to.

4 When you feel ready, simply open your eyes and carry on with your day. If you wish, you can record any experiences you might have had, so that you can read up on them at a later date.

Such occurrences can happen spontaneously when we're feeling down. You may sense that the hug is your deceased loved one acting as your 'guardian angel' from the Other Side. These experiences are always very comforting and loving, and always make you feel better.

Angel blessing

Our angel's unconditional love is always there for the taking. Ask your angel to bring you the feeling of loving support whenever you need help – at any time, no questions asked!

True-life story

Maternal love

I'm going through quite an emotional time at the moment, so I'm doing lots of crying and praying. Just when my heart feels broken to the point where I can't cry any more, a lovely warm feeling always seems to comes over me. I know it's my beautiful mam taking care of me.

Angels of courage

Angels can help us when we feel unwell, lonely or frightened. Just asking for your angels to help you is like calling on a friend. They don't solve every one of life's problems for you, but they can give you the strength you need to deal with the issues yourself. Never think for one minute that your angels are anything less than proud of your efforts. They cheer for you each and every time you handle a problem and solve an issue for yourself. Imagine that they are the friend standing by your side, whispering earnestly, 'Come on, I know you can do it … Keep going, stay strong.' See your angel, in your mind's eye, standing at the end waiting for you when you have completed your goal. Imagine their arms held wide ready to say, 'Congratulations! Well done, I am so proud of you … another goal achieved, another issue dealt with.'

True-life story

Gaining courage from Archangel Michael

When I was in Paris with some colleagues for a weekend, one of them, an ex-boss, kept pushing us to walk around Paris, telling us that she knew the way. It was the hottest day in August and the walk seemed to go on forever, with us never really getting anywhere. Eventually I insisted that we go and sit down for a minute, yet she accused me of being lazy! I got so angry, which was difficult for me because at the time she was my boss. I felt the tears start to prickle on my face, and one of my friends whispered to me to think of my angel. I immediately asked Archangel Michael for assistance and took a few deep breaths. When I felt better we started walking again and, as we turned a corner, I couldn't believe my eyes: there was a huge fountain, with Archangel Michael in the middle! I had shivers down my spine. He gave me courage to call for a taxi and get us out of there.

Angels of protection

In an ideal world we would never put ourselves in positions of danger, but real life means that on occasions we find ourselves accidentally in trouble. It's at times like these that your angels can work at their best. Your guardian angel might lead you to a place of safety, or bring an angel in disguise to take you to a place of protection.

Exercise

Angel protection ritual

1 Imagine your angel is standing over you. He's tall and even a little bit scary – not to you, of course, but to anyone or anything that might put you in harm's way.

2 Archangel Michael is the angel in charge of the heavenly armies. He carries a flaming sword. In your mind's eye, see Michael in his position of power, maybe even wearing armour.

3 If the danger is from other people, ask him to put a protective cloak around you. Stand tall and move yourself out of danger as quickly as possible and with the utmost confidence.

Angels of inspiration

I love it when angels bring me an inspirational thought. It seems to appear as if from nowhere, but always after I've asked for help. My answers usually come to me within the space of a day, and I get a type of 'aha' moment when I am suddenly tuned into their messages.

If you're struggling with a problem, don't forget to ask your angels to help you. You too might feel a cloak of angel inspiration surround you.

Angels of fun

Angels take their human charges very seriously, but they still have a sense of humour. They don't laugh at us, but they love to laugh with us. Angels see humour in every problem and we'd do well to follow their lead.

- Lighten up, when things seem bad; try to see the humour in life as we do.
- Solutions come more easily to your problems when you look on the 'Light' side of life.

We might consider laughing at our own reaction to life when little things go wrong. For a long time I would stamp my feet and swear if I spilt something or broke an object accidentally. Then one day I realized how ridiculous I must have looked – it was as if the angels placed a cartoon image of me having a tantrum. I laughed my head off and, from that moment on, whenever I had a little accident around the house I would simply tidy the broken pieces away or quietly sweep the mess into the waste-paper bin. By getting cross I was only causing myself more anguish and upsetting myself more. In the end, what did my stroppy behaviour achieve? Nothing, so I stopped it.

It's not only when we're cross that we need more humour in our lives. My angels showed me that watching comedy shows on television is a great way to relieve stress. The more I laugh, the better I feel. My baby granddaughter also has me roaring with laugher. And I love it when my two cats chase each other round and round – the little one is better at hiding and always seems to get her own back on the bigger cat, which can be a bit of a bully. There is nothing funnier than watching the smaller cat get the upper hand!

What makes you laugh? Going out with friends? Playing games with your children? Rolling around with the dog? Whatever makes you laugh, do more of it. Make it an angel 'prescription' and take a little laughter each and every day, with a glass of water to help you swallow it!

Angel blessing

When you're feeling down, know that your angels are around as your constant companions and friends. Allow them to bring joy into your life, and know that it gives them great pleasure to see you having fun.

Angels of forgiveness

Forgiveness is a lesson that many of us come to learn in this lifetime. Carrying a grudge against someone who has hurt you is like shooting yourself and expecting the other person to suffer. It makes no sense. Although it's important that the other person atones for their wrongdoing, this is a lesson for their soul, not yours. Your lesson is that you shouldn't carry the pain of the act itself; even better if you can take wisdom from the experience and do something useful with it (for example, help others in a similar situation who've been wronged).

Forgiving a wrongdoing is not easy, but it's quite possible. Make it your ultimate goal. Ask the angels of forgiveness to help you with this challenge. I promise that you'll feel better as forgiveness lifts away the pain of the memory.

Angels of wisdom

We incarnate on Earth to learn many lessons, one of which is wisdom. Traditionally the elders of the pack or tribe were the ones most often blessed with wisdom; the ones who had lived longest on Earth were likely to have learnt this quality and how to use it. Wisdom is about making the right choices – those choices with the best possible outcome for all concerned.

Young children make many mistakes, always following the path of least resistance. To the angels we are all like children, but in a nice way. The angels don't judge the children of God, in the same way that we don't judge our own children. Wisdom is learnt through experience – often the experience of doing things incorrectly. While you are learning this most important of life skills, ask the angels of wisdom to help you make the best choices in your life.

Angel blessing

Make use of the age-old wisdom of the angels to guide you, for they love to assist the human race in this way. Simply ask whenever you feel in need of a little assistance.

Angels of peace

Angels long for peace on Earth. Humankind can seem like warriors to the angels, who are confused and bemused at the way we take to the sword and gun. Killing 'sparks of the God creation' is not the answer to earthly conflict. 'How can I help?' you may ask. Well, start at home, within your own circle of friends and family.

- Smile in greeting to your family, friends and even strangers on the street.
- Start a ripple of happiness everywhere you go with your kind words and actions.
- Try to help someone with a little act of kindness each and every day.
- Treat your pets well. Give them time as you would your human friends. Talk to them, stroke them and tell them how much they mean to you.
- Pay a compliment each day, whenever you think something nice about someone or something; share your thoughts in words.
- Avoid watching the news or reading the paper when you can. Don't allow the stories of war and fighting to enter your reality. Already people around the world are saying, 'No – no more, we want to live in peace!'

After winning the Nobel Peace Prize, Mother Teresa was asked, 'What can we do to promote world peace?' She answered simply, 'Go home and love your family.'

Angels of knowledge

When we finally shed our human bodies and return as a spirit to the heavenly realms we don't take any of our human possessions with us. Everything we learn on Earth, however, is taken as a gift.

Knowledge is a reward that we gain from our lessons here on the Earth plane. Learn well while you are here. Never stop studying this world that we live in. Enjoy your time on Earth and make the most of every second.

There is so much to learn about the Earth. What will you remember most about your life here on this planet? Will you recall the joy you saw when a rainbow appeared in the sky? Will you remember playing with snow, or sitting on a beach or riverbank? Perhaps you'll recall the delight you felt watching plants and flowers grow and bloom?. Take this knowledge about our wonderful Eden with you!

The Book of Records

Every thought, word and deed is recorded in a special place in Heaven called the Book of Records. There are other names for it, and you may have heard of some of them: the Halls of Learning, the Book of Life, the Akashic Records. Would you live your life differently if you knew that your every action was recorded forever? Are there things you wish you had never done, thought or said? I know I have things on my list! We might not be able to change the past, but we can certainly change the way we live in the future. Is it time to make new 'life rules' for yourself? Have a look at the things you would like to do better, then ask the angels of knowledge to help you. Here are a few ideas:

- Try not to judge others for the way they look, sound or feel. Other people make choices based on their own life situations. Without being in their shoes, we have no idea what they base their decisions on.
- Rather than criticize someone for what they are doing wrong, can you help them? Could you be kinder to them?

- Be more tolerant of other people and their actions. People act in the way they do based on outside stimuli, of which again we may have no knowledge.
- Perhaps you would like the angels to help you be more patient.
- How about spending some time teaching others?

Now make your own list.

Angels of communication

Do you talk to your angel? Do you let your angel know that you want to receive communication back? Giving is the best way of receiving.

Many of life's difficulties can be sorted out by sitting down with the other party in question and talking things through. Compromise is the key word, and angels can help you find this. Imagine how we could change the world by talking, not fighting.

When you have challenging situations coming up – such as interviews, or speaking or chatting through problems in public – ask your angel to assist you. This can be especially helpful if you have to do some public speaking or give a presentation. Most of us speak far too fast when we're worried – slow down your speech so that you can hear your angel's reply. Quieten your mind as you await their signals. Take your time and you'll find your talk easier to do. Give yourself thinking time – or listening time – to tune into your angels.

Communication is all about balance. I heard a great saying once: 'Two ears for hearing, one mouth for speaking – use them in proportion.' Isn't that brilliant?

Angel blessing

Relax, and allow your angels to assist you when you need to speak out about things that are important to you. Your angels can help bring you courage to manifest your words.

- *We can be your words, if you listen to our guidance.*

True-life stories

Everyday contact

I say hello to my angel every morning, and every morning without fail I feel a warm hug, which starts at my spine and wraps itself around my shoulders, arms and chest.

Angels of healing

My books are full of stories of angels healing human beings, as well as saving lives. If it's not 'your time' to leave the Earth plane of existence, they can perform miracles of care, as many people tell me.

Angels love to watch over their human charges in this way. The angel in charge of healing is the great Archangel Raphael (see page 29). When you're in pain, at the doctor, dentist or in hospital, ask Raphael to sit beside you holding your hand.

Know that you are not alone and that he is working on your body from the inside out.

True-life story

A helping hand

I feel the hand of my angel on my shoulder a lot. It's a difficult time in my life right now and I get great comfort from knowing she's around me. I feel warm on the side of my body that she touches – always my left side, and always when I need it most. Life just wouldn't be the same without my angel.

Angel blessing

God has created angels of healing. When you need a little assistance with your physical or mental body, call upon the angels to help you heal and realign into perfect health.

Working with the angels on your health

Allow the angels to help work on your bodily healing. Give them permission by lying or sitting in a comfortable position, then feel the angelic healing light as it floods through your body. Relaxing is the key to angel healing. Your loving angels may say to you:

• Taking care of your body is something we do together. Let's co-create the perfect shell for your soul to reside in, each of us doing our part to manifest perfect health.

Working on human health is a two-way thing. We work alongside the angels. It's no good eating excessive animal fats or sugars, drinking too much alcohol or smoking, and then moaning about the state of your body. The angels do their part, but so much is up to you. Here are some reminders of what the angels are requesting of us:

• Take some exercise every day.
• Walk out in nature as often as you can.
• When you can't be in the countryside, bring the countryside to you and surround yourself with plants, flowers, crystals and water.
• Take care of your body by eating as healthily as you can. Treats are still permitted, of course, but don't eat so that you feel out of control. You should rule your food decisions and not let your body do so! Be awake to your choices.

- Spend some time relaxing.
- Eat fresh, natural foods, and reduce (or give up) as many processed foods as you can.
- If you're adding poisons to your body, like alcohol and cigarettes, ask your doctor to help you cut down – or preferably give up – on these substances (don't make these changes alone; always work with your health adviser to ensure you are making the changes safely). Ask the Archangel Raphael to support these changes.
- Allow a little time each day for meditation and contemplation. Let your mind switch off from its daily influences, to better connect with your inner world and that of the angels.

Angels of creation (manifesting)

Our Creator God provides everything we need – although not everything we want, perhaps! Stay positive at all times, to manifest the things you need into your life. Create visualizations, draw the physical objects you require, or cut out images from magazines and stick them on your pinboard or frame them. Know that they are already in your life waiting for you to create them on the physical plane.

True-life story
Angelic gifts

A few weeks ago I went to a shop to buy some medicine and, while I was waiting to pay, a feather came down from above and fell next to my feet. Yesterday morning when I got up I found two very dainty feathers in my bedroom, and when I cleaned my cupboard I found the most beautiful guinea-fowl feather in one of my shoeboxes.

This morning I found a bead next to my bed, in the shape of a pearl and gold in colour. I have been battling with depression lately, and have been asking the angels for help and encouragement and to show me how I can get back to my old self again. Clearly they are giving me signs that they are with me, and it is a big comfort to know that I am not alone.

I am keeping all the feathers and have decided to make sun-catchers with beads and feathers for all my friends and family, and will attach a message to all of them.

Exercise

Loving energy manifestation

During your creative endeavours, ask the angels to help you create that magic in your life using everyday objects. Hold the feeling of love and peace in your heart – it's no more difficult than feeling sorry for yourself, I promise! Let's give it a go …

1 Stop whatever you are doing right now. Close your eyes and imagine a bright-yellow beam of love, peace and happiness entering your heart and, as it does so, flooding your whole body.

2 Let these wonderful feelings fill every corner of your body, including your fingers, toes and even behind your ears! It's a strange thing to do, isn't it? Funny even.

3 Enjoy the sensation, and let any negativity that is hiding in these corners of your body simply float away, washed out by the yellow light. You might even feel a shiver or a light vibration as you do this.

Angels of comfort

When angels appear to comfort us, they usually do so in disguised form. Your angel might appear to you in a variety of ways, including some of the following:

• A human friend is momentarily guided by the inner voice of an angel to say words that you need to hear, or to help you in the way you most need.
• A pet jumps up on your lap or comes over for a hug, knowing that you require angel support.
• A stranger appears out of the blue to assist you.
• Butterflies, birds, dragonflies and other creatures appear when least expected, or act in unusual ways to indicate the presence of a loved one or angel nearby.
• A light or a scent lets you know that your loved ones or angels are with you. Flowers are a common scent, but you might pick up the smell of

great-granddad's tobacco, or even grandma's chocolate cake! Have you ever had reassurance like this come through to you?

True-life story
Butterfly surprise

Last August my mom passed away very suddenly. I was shocked and, being the youngest, it was very hard on me. At the wake there was a reddish-brownish butterfly flying around the room near the coffin, which my family saw, but as I wasn't present at the time I missed it. I was pretty upset I didn't get to see it because I knew it was a sign from my mom.

Three months ago, while I was in the living room, the same-coloured butterfly appeared and, believe it or not, stayed in that room for almost a week. I would go in and see it every day, and no one in the family saw it but me. Then it disappeared and I searched everywhere in that room and the other rooms in the house, but it was nowhere to be seen. Then around three weeks later the same butterfly appeared in the same room, in the same place! Again no one else but me saw it. I felt it was my mom letting me know she was there, because everyone else had seen the butterfly at the wake, except me.

True-life story
Roses of love

My mum died in January 2008, and as it was the year that she and Dad would have been married for 60 years, he had 60 red roses put on her coffin.

The day after her funeral I was driving home from their house, prior to going to hospital for a mammogram, and suddenly the car was filled with an overpowering scent of roses. My daughter was in the car with me and she could smell it, despite having a rotten cold and a severely bunged-up nose. The scent stayed with us all the way home. Sadly, the mammogram showed that I was ill and needed surgery.

The day I went into hospital for the operation I was sitting in the waiting room of the Transitional Care Unit with just my husband present in the room, when suddenly we were surrounded by the scent of flowers. I'm sure it was my mum letting me know that she was there with me, and I did see her later on that evening when I awoke after the surgery. She was standing there beside my bed.

The right angel, right now

Have a think about the type of angel you need in your life right now. There are angels for everything you require. If you know the angel in charge of a particular area, or an angel with the skill or knowledge that you need, you can call upon them specifically. If not, then it's okay just to ask for 'the right angel' to help you. Know that it will be done.

Find us in every flower, every tree, and even in the sky and the earth. Know that we, your angels, are always around you.

Angel inspiration

Allow us to inspire you in your daily life; just ask for our help

One of the ways in which angels communicate with us is by bringing us inspirational thoughts. I often ask for help from my angels, with no clear goal in mind. Sometimes this is easier for the angels! Let them help you in their own way. Often the ideas that angels suggest are far better than the ones we could think of on our own.

Angels can see the bigger picture. They have a wider view of what is going on in our lives and can see brilliant ways of helping us. Sometimes the angels' ideas may be more dramatic than our own, but they seem to know what they are doing. If you've been messing around in a pointless career that makes you feel miserable, the angels will help you move on. Ask for their help in your mind, ask out loud or even write your request in a little note. Of course the ideal outcome is that someone approaches you with a perfect job all lined up and ready to go. Instead, however, the angels might:

- Bring an end to your job in a sudden way to force you to find new work.
- Arrange for a change in your personal circumstances so that you are compelled to search out work in a new part of the country or in another part of the world.

- Modify your situation so that you have to find a way of altering the hours that you work.
- Present a new opportunity whereby you have to retrain or study for an exam of some sort.
- Bring someone into your life who is looking for a new employee with the exact skill-set that you have.

Angel blessing

The angels help us to be gainfully employed either by earning our living or by using our time in a way that is fulfilling to us. Ask the angels to assist you in creating the life you wish for; then follow their lead as they bring you signs to direct you to the correct path.

Exercise
Manifestation ritual

For this ritual you'll need a small, smooth crystal. If you have some at home, you can select one from your collection; if not, you'll find 'tumbled crystals' (ones with all the rough edges smoothed away in a 'tumbling machine') in your local New Age store or gift shop (or try the internet). Choose a crystal specifically for the purpose of bringing something into your life. If you can't find a crystal, then you can use a pebble instead.

1 Draw a picture of your heart's desire, or use a postcard, or cut a photograph from a magazine to represent whatever you want to introduce into your life. Maybe you want the angels to help you become pregnant or adopt a child, bring you the money to pay a bill, or find you a new job.

2 Place your chosen crystal and your picture in a little drawstring bag or pouch.

3 Now write the following words onto a slip of paper: 'Powerful and majestic angels, who art from up above. Please help to manifest my wish, and bring it to me with love.' If you wish, you can use a metallic pen, or write on a pretty piece of paper, in order to give the ritual greater importance.

4 To let your angels bring the goal about in their own way, include the following phrase at the end of your note: 'This or something better'.

5 Sign your name and include the words 'Thank you'.

6 Read the words out from your slip of paper once you've written them, then add it to the pouch.

7 Place the bag under your pillow or beneath your bed. Leave it there until your desire has been accomplished. Remember to follow the clues and directions that the angels bring you – be alert to this; look for their signs.

Inspirational 'shower'

When we ask angels for inspiration, their messages can be received in many different ways. They may arrange for us to bump into an old friend who will bring us a message, or perhaps the message will come to us in a dream (many of my own contacts come this way).

My favourite way of being inspired is by receiving an angel 'shower' of information! Minutes after your request – or maybe hours or days – inspiration will come to you all at once. Words are not necessary, as you suddenly know the truth that you have been waiting for. It's as if the angels have waved a magic wand over you, and you feel excited as many ideas buzz around your brain at once. An inspirational shower of information from the angels will wash over you; you'll almost feel giddy with emotion and will want to start work on the ideas right away.

If you need help in any situation, just keep asking the angels, for it's amazing what they can do on our behalf. Watch out for inspirational showers occurring to you as you read this book.

True-life story
Abundant work

I do driving work, and have been doing so for more than ten years now. Once I ran out of work, and I was desperate as I needed money to cover some bills. I put out a request to my angels, asking for abundance in the way the organization that I drive for thinks about me for work. I waited two weeks and suddenly I was overwhelmed with driving work. Ask your angels – it does work.

True-life story
Angel fire officers

A few years ago I went on holiday in June and asked Archangel Michael to protect the house while we were away. I thought nothing of it until months later a neighbour was chatting with me and talked about the fire next door to my house. I asked her what she was talking about, and she told me that the young people had a party next door and left the chip-fryer on, which happened to have a bottle of white spirit next to it. It caught light. However, the fire burnt itself out, never leaving the kitchen. Apparently the firemen told my neighbour that someone must have been watching over them as he had never seen a fire do that, and it should have taken out next door (my house) as well. I asked when this happened and she said, 'Last June!'

Creating sacred space near water

Being around water can help amplify your angelic connections. Of course, sitting beside the rolling waves, walking along a riverbank or meditating by a waterfall has to represent the A+ of sacred spots for angel interaction; while I am lucky enough to live by the sea, I realize that not everyone has access to such places every day, which is a shame, for the 'negative ions' (despite their name) have a positive effect on our health, as was first documented in a scientific paper in 1892. A walk in the fresh country air or sitting next to a large fountain can work in a similar way. Being close to running water can help lift depression, too.

It's been shown that the air around Niagara Falls contains between 30,000 and 100,000 negative ions per cubic centimetre. In comparison, the average office environment or sealed car typically contains anywhere between zero and a few hundred negative ions per cubic centimetre.

Running water of any sort is useful, so why not make use of your bathroom? I've lost count of the number of people who have written and shared angelic experiences they have had while showering or taking a bath. You can steal a little showering time to simply 'be', and ask your angels to reach out to you at these times. Partly this happens because of the relaxation you can achieve, and partly because of the closeness of the running water to you. If you prefer a bath to a shower, that's fine, too: try to sit in the bath as the water is filling the tub and soak up the negative ions from the water pouring through the tap.

Crystals, candles and scented oils can all help your experience feel more sacred and magical. One candle is probably plenty – more can look pretty, but breathing in lots of smoke is not really helpful!

Here are some ideas to enhance your sacred bathroom space:

• Add a figurine of an angel, faeries (nature's angels), mermaids (part of the nature realms) or goddess-type figures.

- Add a plant or two (this not only helps to oxygenate the space, but makes you feel more as if you're outdoors in nature). Most of us aren't going to be bathing in a waterfall in a jungle, but we can bring hanging or climbing plants into the space, to look at while we shower.
- Choose a large, clear, pointed quartz crystal or a substantial piece of pointed amethyst and sit it on the windowsill or, if you have space, at the end of the bath.
- Add a large shell full of natural soaps (seaside stores sell these, if you can't find one in your part of the world). Alternatively, look for a rustic open bowl to pile your natural goodies in.
- Use a natural sponge.
- Put a chunky church-type candle (a plain cream one) in a dish/holder on a flat surface or on a windowsill (make sure it's in a safe place, where it won't be knocked over or blown out) – preferably somewhere you can see it while you bathe.
- Work with the colours of nature: soft blues and greens. My bathroom has a pottery angel holding a moulded shell-shape for a tea-light – blue to match the colours of the room. Harmony helps create peace. If your suite is white, you'll have even more choice.

Indoor water feature

Water features do take a little effort to maintain, but the soothing sound of running water is really relaxing to listen to and perfect in a space where you may meditate. The more you can relax, the closer to your angel friends you can get. You can have a water feature in your kitchen (if you have enough space) or next to a place where you relax. Make sure you top up the water regularly – your local aquarium shop will suggest suitable water cleaners and purifiers. Ensure it is pet-safe if your feature is within reach of animals.

I've recently introduced a water feature into my meditation/writing room at home. It sits on the windowsill behind my desk. I've chosen something that looks like natural rock and have decorated it with a few crystals (which help to amplify the natural energy created by the water feature). I've also added a few pennies around the edge of the water fountain – a symbolic way of expressing thanks for the energy (an 'energy exchange', or payment for services offered). To make my water feature

seem more natural I have surrounded it with lush green houseplants. It uplifts me both to look at it and to listen to it! The plants love the negative ions too. And of course there is an angel figurine standing regally over my water feature. Faeries, being nature energies, are equally appropriate as decoration for your indoor arrangement.

Meditations done at your water feature can be quite intense, for it is already a place of peace and positive energies.

Water altar

If a water circulator is out of your budget at the moment, put it on your Christmas or birthday list. You can even make your own using a small pump (ask for advice at your local aquatic centre). In the meantime, fill a shallow bowl full of water and put a few pieces of natural rose quartz (still in their rough shape) at the bottom of the bowl. Add this to the centre of your angel altar and surround it with plants. Keep the water fresh by changing it every couple of days. The water will evaporate into the air and help counteract the drying effects of living in a centrally heated home.

A water altar works really well in a conservatory. Just stand a shallow plant saucer on the floor, or on a low plastic crate or a water-safe surface, if you want to raise it up a bit. As long as you keep the water fresh (and the crystals not too small), it doesn't matter if your pets sneak a drink! Disguise a plastic bowl by surrounding it with large plants for a verdant and flourishing jungle-like feel, giving a fantastic energy to your room. Decorate it with clip-on butterfly decorations (you'll find these in gift shops and garden centres, being sold as Christmas-tree decorations).

You can also hang a few plants from the ceiling in knotted rope (macramé) hangers. Go on, get carried away! How about adding a few pretty rocks from the garden, or some dry pieces of bark? When you've finished, throw a cushion on the floor to sit on, and call in your angels.

Finding room for such spaces in your home is especially important if you live in a town, or if your health means you are unable to leave your house very much. If you can't get out into nature, bring nature home to you. You'll love finding new ways of stimulating the senses to create an inner harmony.

Salt lamps

Salt-crystal rocks can be bought as 'salt lamps'. A 'well' is hollowed out of one end to create space for a bulb or candle, so that it can be lit from the inside. The lamp gives off an attractive glow, which makes it suitable for use as a night-light or for creating a relaxing atmosphere. Salt crystal is a soft material that is easily carved, and the rough shapes have many variations. It's a beautiful addition to your meditation space.

I have one right behind my computer. The ambient air surrounding a 'salt lamp' is cleaned by the transformation cycle of hydrogen and oxygen, as well as by sodium and chloride ions. Many believe it to be helpful for relieving the symptoms associated with asthma and allergies in general. Rock-salt lamps, like running water, release negative ions into the atmosphere. I'm now surrounded: a water feature behind my desk and a salt lamp in front!

Although the effects are not fully understood, office workers suffering from health complaints blamed on fluorescent lighting and computer monitors report experiencing less fatigue and fewer headaches if the negative ions in the air around them are increased.

Recycle or reuse

There are many suggestions for purchases in this book, but don't feel that you need all or any of them to connect to your angels. I often look for recycled items, or natural objects that I can put together myself. And it's highly likely that you'll already have objects in your home that you can put to a new use. (On the other hand, if you want to purchase something new and need an excuse for buying, by all means blame me!)

Now I've suggested that you recommission items from around your home, here are a few ideas for you (no doubt you'll think of lots more of your own):

- You can make your altar cloth out of an old silk scarf.
- A bread basket is a great place to store your angel cards and books – I use baskets for just about everything!
- Some candles come in glasses. I clean out the glasses after use, removing any remaining wax with a kitchen knife, and then pour hot water inside and polish them with a piece of kitchen paper. You can then decorate

them with glass paints or glitter, or leave them plain and reuse them as tea-light holders (I even use some as drinking glasses).

- Gather feathers when you next go out for a walk. Small white fluffy ones can be added to greetings cards or letters, or given to friends as angel gifts when they need a little support. Longer feathers can be bundled together. Use your feather bundles to 'smudge' the smoke from incense or dried sage. Sage smoke is traditionally used to cleanse a person, aura or room.
- Collect shells and pretty stones or pebbles to use in your inside or outside angel displays and altars.
- Save Christmas cards illustrated with angels and use them throughout the year for angel crafts.
- Remove seasonal trimmings and reuse your angel Christmas ornaments all year round.

Unclogging the energy channels

As well as the pollution surrounding us in our cities and towns, the foods and other substances that we consume can block angelic contact. In biblical times angels seemed ever-present, but then people didn't eat food from packets and jars! The chemicals that we add to our food to preserve them can sometimes cause unwanted side-effects in our bodies. While our ability to preserve foods has had a positive effect on our lives (fruit that was once available only in the summer is now available all year round as jam, for instance), the actual products that we use to preserve foods can be harmful.

Sugar and salt, and preservatives that are synthesized artificially, can cause allergic reactions and a wide range of disorders, including high blood pressure, gastrointestinal distress, abdominal cramping and fatigue. Our bodies are constantly battling with these additives. For instance, psoriasis is much improved when processed foods are eliminated from the diet.

The fewer processed foods we eat (foods full of sugar, fat, salt and chemicals), the clearer and less clogged-up our channels to higher-energy beings become. The problem with many of these types of foods is that we find them irresistible. We crave foods with salt and sugar in particular – and manufacturers know this. If you fall into this category, look for extra help to withdraw from these addictive foods. The trick is to remove one item at a time. Never change your diet completely overnight, as the withdrawal symptoms that the body suffers can be equally dangerous. Seek assistance from your doctor, or find a nutritionist to assist you.

Aim to remove one addictive food every month or so and, as you do so, increase your water intake. The amount you need to drink varies throughout the world, depending on many things, including the weather. In the UK the National Health Service website suggests drinking six to eight glasses of fluid a day, and slightly more in hot weather, if you are exercising more (around an extra 1 litre/1¾ pint for each hour of exercise) or if you are unwell. Look for the suggested daily amount in your part of the world.

Drugs, nicotine and alcohol can also block the energy channels, but again don't suddenly stop taking prescriptive medicines and don't change your smoking or drinking habits drastically overnight without working alongside a trained specialist or doctor. You can always ask your doctor if other treatments are available to you, or if a change of lifestyle might enable you to reduce (or even stop taking) certain types of medicine. For example, high blood pressure and diabetes can be improved in some cases by changing your diet and by losing weight. High blood pressure can occur for many different reasons, however, so help your health professional to discover the reason for yours. Always work with medical support and professional advice.

Regular exercise and low-fat, low-sugar, low-salt diets containing lots of fresh fruit, vegetables and salad make plain good sense. To increase your ability to perceive and connect with other realms and dimensions, watch what you put into your body!

Exercise

Physical cleansing meditation

Most meditations take place when the body is quiet and sitting, kneeling or lying down. This one is a little different in that you will be standing and moving slightly. You'll still need to relax, though, so music is important.

1 Dress in loose, flowing clothes. If you own Indian-style long cotton skirts or flowing scarves, this is the time to wear them! You'll want to be barefoot too, so if you're outside make sure you're standing on something smooth – perhaps a grassed area.

2 Set up your music. Look for something without words, maybe a gentle classical piece or something New Age or angel-like. It may be a little faster than you'd normally use for meditation.

3 Find a space where you have plenty of room to move about. If you have nosy neighbours you may prefer to push the furniture back to the corners of your living room and work inside instead.

4 Now set your music playing, then start swaying backwards and forwards in time to the music. When your body feels a little more relaxed you can begin moving in a figure-of-eight shape. Make your shape as big as you can, so that you don't feel dizzy. The figure eight is the symbol of eternity – a continuous loop.

5 When your legs have warmed up a little, start moving your arms. Sway them gently at first and then lift them up into the air as if you were offering a sacrifice to the angels (you're not sacrificing yourself to anything, so don't panic!).

6 Now take one arm and circle it over your head. Bring it up in front of you, circle it round to the back and then flick your hand away from you, as if you were brushing something away. Do the same thing with the other hand in the opposite direction. Repeat several times, slowly and with deliberate intent.

7 Join your hands in front of you in a big hoop shape and draw the hoop over your head. Then release your hands, cross them over your head and, as you uncross them, sweep your hands down in front of your body, crossing them back again as they get close to your feet, and finishing by touching the floor. Repeat the same sweeping motion on each side of your body, touching the floor after each movement.

8 Swing your right arm behind you as if you were brushing a cobweb off your clothes, and then swivel around so that you can touch the floor behind you. Do the same with the left arm. This all seems really complicated, but I promise it's a lot easier than it sounds. Get a friend to read this to you as you do the actions (then swap over). Next time you'll do it without help.

9 Continue swaying your arms gently in time to the music until you reach the end of the track. Right at the end make one complete circle and, if you wish, finish with your hands in a praying position.

10 Now allow the angels to inspire you.

We, your angels have the power to lift and enhance the energy that surrounds you. Listen as we whisper words of advice to uplift the world around you.

Dream-work and spirit guides

*We know you cannot always see
us during your waking hours,
so we try to bring you messages
and signs when you are asleep*

When people write to me they assume I can see angels with my physical eyes. Sadly, for most people this is not the case, and even I rarely see them with my own eyes. My angels mainly appear to me when I am asleep … and I love it that way! It's the least frightening method for them to communicate with us, and I encourage it whenever I can.

Before I go to sleep, I ask them, 'Please angels, bring me inspirational messages and words of wisdom.' Sometimes I'll ask the angels if I can go and visit with them. I rarely see them this way but often when deceased relatives come to visit me in dreams, the angels and guides are there, waiting patiently in the background, offering a boost of energy to enable the visit to occur.

Angel blessing

The angels often see a little way ahead, into possible future outcomes. Ask your angels to help you bring about the best scenario possible and to guide you in the right direction to create this angel blessing.

Future signs

Angels bring messages and signs that they are around me, and sometimes they bring inspiration and ideas for the projects I'm working on. If I'm really lucky they introduce insights about things that are going to happen in my future.

Of course the future is not set in stone – it's not fixed – but we have a great deal of influence on what is going to happen to us in the life ahead. So in most cases the 'future' is the most likely outcome based on the current set of circumstances. You, naturally, can change that current set of circumstances. In nearly every situation, your life is literally in your own hands.

Do you realize how much control you have over your future? Even when negative things 'happen' to us, we get to choose how we feel about it. Bring your attention to the now. Live each moment as if it were all you had. You choose how that now exists. Make a choice that is in harmony with your best life, something that works with your health and well-being. Choose to feel good. Choose to feel happy. Choose to feel joy and peace, ignoring outside influences that might affect you in a negative way. Simply imagine yourself 'switching off' that negative button and 'switching on' the voice within that reminds you, 'What did I choose to learn? Why did I pick this opportunity in my life?'

Often when things go 'wrong' (or what we perceive as wrong) this is an opportunity in disguise, and our angels know this. When we're on the wrong path and not paying attention, they may instigate things that scare us initially – things that will help to push us on our correct path. Here are a couple of examples:

Negative experience: You feel a deep dread at going to work each day. You're unhappy with your work and everything about the place.

Positive outcome: This 'feeling' is an indication that you need to change your job! Your vibrational energy has changed and you no longer 'fit'. I know it sounds obvious, but how many people stick with the same job they hate for months, or even years? Are you scared about moving on? Of course you are, but you know you'll not be alone. Your angel will be by your side every step of the way.

Nothing you do now is going to make you feel worse than you already do. So the future is in your hands. You can stay and receive more of the same, or leave and change the future. To feel more comfortable, find a job with an energy that vibrates at a rate that is close to your own. Ask your angels to help you. If you want to work with fun, happy and positive people, then ask your angels to help attract a job that will bring you these things.

Negative experience: You've always talked about living by the beach, and yet here you are, getting on with your life and still living in the middle of a town that you hate! You feel miserable every day.

Positive outcome: To find the peace you seek, you have to decide either: a) that you want to achieve this goal really badly and are prepared to do whatever it takes to create this situation in your life; or b) that you will come to terms with the idea that you are actually happy where you are, or you would have done something about it by now! Either way, change how you feel about it to create the positive outcome.

Doing 'whatever it takes' might include:

* Selling your home
* Downsizing
* Giving away or selling some possessions
* Giving up a relationship
* Changing your job
* Living on less money
* Rehoming pets
* Helping relatives or friends who live
  with you to find new accommodation

Do something different

Change is always scary, because we are frightened things won't work out, but if you long to live in a certain place or want to be with someone very badly, then achieving your goal might mean that you no longer need all the other things in your life and that you have to make the changes. Moving away from family and friends (even temporarily) to achieve your goals can be challenging. You need to give yourself at least 12 months before you can say, 'Well, that didn't work.' It takes time to adjust.

There is a saying, 'If you want to achieve the same results, keep doing the same things.' I couldn't put it better myself. To achieve change in your life, do something different. No one ever got to their deathbed and regretted the things they tried that didn't work out, but many people regret the things they never tried. You can always change your mind again!

I lost a dear friend recently. Her passing was unexpected, as she was only 59. I looked at my own life and had many questions. Have I done everything I want to do? If not, why not? There was only one answer: write a list and start ticking things off. Begin making plans today!

Dream help: Write down your request for help before you go to bed, explaining what you want in your life. Add it to your angel journal. Watch for dream clues or even a real visit from your angel or guide, offering wise words of assistance.

Angel blessing

Angels work in the light, the highest possible vibration. Ask your angels to help take your thoughts to the highest possible vibration too — look to the light, and see things only in a positive way.

True-life story
Angelic help

I wear my late mother's necklace every day. It has an angel charm attached to it and it's really special to me. One day I'd been messing about with the chain, which was hanging alongside my dog whistle around my neck. They both got mixed up with my long hair and there was a major 'tangle' going on. My dad and my friend Clare tried to untangle it, but sadly to no avail.

Clare said, 'Lindy, I'm sorry, but I can't get it untangled and I think it's going to break. It's really bad.' I had been holding my angel charm throughout this 'nightmare' and decided to speak to my angels in my mind. 'Please can you help me?' I asked them. Clare said the knot instantly untangled in her hands, and my dad looked on in amazement. There wasn't even any of my hair attached to my necklace or the angel charm!

I was so very happy as I didn't wish my mum's chain to break. I did thank the angels following my plea for help.

Reminder message

Although we have touched on this already in the book, here is the most important message I have for you, so let's repeat it: your subconscious cannot differentiate between positive and negative thoughts, and works hard to create that which you think about most. Concentrate, therefore, on thinking about the things you want to manifest in your life. Talk only about the positive things you wish to bring into your reality, rather than any negative feelings you carry. Your subconscious will bring into your life those thoughts (things) that you concentrate on most, so why constantly mull over the things that annoy you?

As always, ask your angels to help you begin practising this new way of thinking. Think positive thoughts – we'll do another reminder later on.

How the angels help you

As we now know, if you ask your angels for help, they don't always come up with the idea that you might have considered yourself. Their help may not be what you want, but it's probably what you need.

When I ask my angels a question about the future, they often give me the answer 'It's up to you' in my dreams, which suggests that I am the master/mistress of my own fate. That's an interesting concept. Will I succeed or fail? Will I be happy or sad? Will I move house or stay put? Will I change my job and retrain for something new or stay where I am? So much of life is in our own hands. The angels will help us on the path that we decide on – we are the planners and the angels are the ones who cheer us on, leading us to the right people and helping us to be in the right place to achieve our goals.

Can you hear your angel's whispered voice? Does this comment strike a chord inside you? Choose to succeed! Don't sit back moaning about it – take action. Do something today.

Angel blessing

Your angels are always working behind the scenes to help you manifest your dreams and your chosen life path. Know that they are always supporting your choices and ensuring that your life does not come into conflict with your pre-life plans and goals.

True-life story

Surrounded by love

I am lucky enough to be able to see and hear my angels and guides. They bring me inspired thoughts and images; it can be different each time. With my angels I can either see their image or sometimes a colour. I always feel them when they are around: it is an overwhelming feeling of love that surrounds me, and at times it can even bring tears to my eyes. Very occasionally I hear their voices, but usually I am given inspired thoughts in a very gentle voice.

Getting angels to appear in dreams

Like all angel work, it's important that you give your angels permission to appear to you in a dream. Don't expect that your angel will always look like a traditional winged angel when it enters your dream. You may assume that a being with a halo will manifest before you, but often my own angels and guides look nothing like that in dreams. They appear as normal human beings, bringing me information, sometimes in parable or story form. I often have to work out the relevance of the message – they like us to do some of the work!

On occasions your 'angel' may be a deceased loved one. Relatives and friends who have passed away can be the perfect messengers. Our reunions may be emotional ones, even when we are asleep. When a deceased loved one walks into your dream – sometimes quite literally walks (or floats) – it's common for the dream to become lucid. A lucid dream is one in which you are aware that your body is asleep, yet your mind is aware and awake. The connection seems real to you; of course it is real! The dreamtime experience may be more vivid than any you have previously experienced.

The reunion may prompt tears of joy, and the phrase 'Why are you here – you're dead, aren't you?' is a common one. When you awake, those tears of happiness may still be lying on your cheeks. The experience will often be recalled in minute detail and can be remembered for many years to come.

Sometimes the detail of the message may be completely forgotten. If you've had this experience, don't be concerned. The information will be buried deep in your subconscious and recalled when you most need it. We still have to work out personally the situations in our earthly life so that our spirit can learn and grow. The angels – and your deceased loved ones – will be helping out too. You are never left to flounder alone.

Our deceased loved ones have limited powers. There are only certain things they are allowed to do, but my experience suggests that they often overstep those boundaries, mainly in a good way. For example, if you planned to break your leg at this stage in your life because your spirit felt it would help you learn the lesson of patience, they might warn you at the pivotal moment, because they realize that a twisted ankle might work just as well. Perhaps you have already done rather well with this lesson and only need a 'top-up' experience to complete the class.

Our angels, guides and deceased loved ones can affect minute changes – adjustments to our 'blueprint'. Dreams are one of the ways in which they do this.

Angel blessing

Know that your deceased loved ones and angels can appear in dreams to communicate with you. If you'd like this experience yourself, then remember to ask. Continue to ask each night until it happens – be patient! They need you to be at a certain level of consciousness to do this and it may take a while to catch you in the right state. Once it happens to you, you'll be amazed. Nothing will ever seem the same again, and you'll know that the phenomenon is 100 percent real. Be prepared to be changed forever.

Working with crystals and angels

Why not pick up a small crystal (clear quartz is ideal) or, if you have a little more cash, a clear-quartz angel figurine. Place it in a small drawstring bag and hang in on your bed or place it under your pillow. Dedicate it as your sleep communication angel, and hold it when you ask your angels to visit you in your dreams. You don't need to spend lots of money on new crystals; if you already have special crystal angels or small tumbled crystals that you use and that feel 'right' to you, use them. The crystals and angels that you have and already love will work just as well.

The best angel dreams and message dreams come when you wake up after a good night's sleep and fall asleep again – this is a magical message time. Why not create this situation by setting your alarm a little earlier than usual? When you wake up, set your alarm again and go back to sleep. See if you can have a visitation in the mysterious space in between.

Dream-sleep crystals

Each crystal has a unique vibration, a unique energy, and this can affect your dreams, especially with dream-visitations. Try some of the crystals suggested below, perhaps one at a time, to see how they affect your own dreams and your dream recall. Do they help angels to connect with you?

You may find that different crystals work for you, and that's fine. Keep a note of the crystals you try so that you can refer back to it. Maybe you can use a specific notebook for this purpose.

Some gift shops sell crystals very cheaply, so start off with the more common ones. Here are a few to try:

- Clear quartz
- Turquoise
- Tiger's eye
- Amethyst
- Celestite

It doesn't matter what size of crystal you use. Small crystals work just as well as big ones. In fact, sometimes smaller crystals can be more useful – you can pop one or two into your pocket or handbag and carry their energy around with you.

Crystal dream: danburite

Many years ago, just after I had published my first book, I was working at a large castle selling angel gifts and teaching some workshops. Another stallholder had a selection of crystals for sale, and I was immediately attracted to a clear stone with a stratified texture. The crystal seemed to be formed in layers or bands and had a frosted, glassy appearance.

Danburite's natural colours are white/clear, but it can also be found in the palest pink. The crystal expert told me that it was a crystal used for working with angels, so no wonder I was attracted to it. A quick internet search when I got home showed me that it can help with stress. According to some reports, danburite opens your crown chakra (the energy centre over your head) and helps stimulate creativity and thought, enabling energy to flow more freely. It also has strong detoxifying and healing qualities.

I had my piece of danburite on display for many years and then, when we moved house, it was tucked away along with my other crystals in plastic divider boxes (tool/craft boxes). Recently I've been feeling out of sorts and I had a dream which suggested that I get out my collection of crystals and put them on display. A couple of days later I was drawn to separate my danburite and place it on an angel-wings dish in front of my computer keyboard.

For the life of me I couldn't remember what the crystal was called, but the very next day I was on Facebook when a photograph of a very large crystal appeared. I was attracted to the crystal and clicked on the image to have a closer look. It was a large piece of amethyst – gorgeous! I wondered if the lady had other photos of crystals, so I moved on to the next shot in her album – it was a large angel figurine holding a crystal that I recognized, and underneath the photo was the word 'danburite'. YES! Seven years after I had purchased the crystal, and one day after I had asked what it was called, I 'coincidentally' came across the name by accident.

I picked up my crystal, mesmerized. I did feel out of balance and, if I'm honest, a little grumpy, so I instinctively popped the crystal inside my clothing. I didn't think about it as I carried on my work and then, almost exactly an hour later, I realized that I felt better. Was it a coincidence? I have no idea.

A couple of days later I was feeling really unbalanced again. Now I am really careful about the types of food that I eat, but I was craving sugar and found myself in the kitchen creating a chocolate-sponge pudding with custard sauce (something I hadn't made for years). I knew the likelihood of feeling bad later on was fairly high, but a little while later I discovered a packet of cream biscuits in the cupboard and managed to munch my way through them too. I never eat biscuits, so what was the matter with me? I don't even like them that much. Sugar really messes up my body balance and, as predicted, I felt unwell almost immediately and it went on for several hours. It was only at that point that I decided to ask my angels for help.

It was nearly bedtime, and as I was getting ready for bed I remembered the crystal again. I walked downstairs to my writing room to collect the danburite and carried it back up to bed. I had no idea what I was going to do with it, but instinctively I tucked it under my pillow. And do you know what? I had a great night's sleep. I woke up in the morning feeling fantastic! My hormonal imbalance had gone, and I had no sugar cravings and no more unwell feelings. It was as if the angels had used the crystals to work on my body as I slept. I even felt detoxified.

Was the angel crystal a miracle cure or a coincidence? I'll leave you to decide that one, but I do believe our angels can help us using these natural tools. Your angels will guide you every step of the way, so just ask them for their help and then be guided by intuition – your angels' way of leading you to the things you need to help you in your life. Let your angels light the way.

Angel blessing

The Earth is full of wonderful tools to help you on your spiritual journey. Look around you and discover beautiful plants and herbs, natural aromatherapy oils and crystals. Feel blessed at the choice nature has to offer, and ask your angels to help lead you to the gifts that can best assist you.

Spirit guides

We all have our very own guardian angels, but did you know you have a spirit guide as well? Angels are beings of light working directly with the God energy. Spirit guides are often souls who have previously lived earthly lives – they have a different energy from angels and are able to communicate with us in human-type ways. A spirit guide is a disincarnated spirit who acts as a guide to a living incarnated human being. Your spirit guide helps by watching, teaching, healing and helping you on your physical journey into spiritual awareness.

My own guides often bring messages to me in dreams, but they may also make themselves known to you by:

• Touching your hand in comfort
• Placing a hand upon your shoulder when you feel sad or alone
• Bringing a sensation like 'cobwebs' around your face
• Moving your hair (mine seem to make the top of my hair move up and down – I can feel it, and even see it happening in the mirror)

Some people's guides can be very specific when communicating with them – they work out a series of signals that mean different things to them.

Spirit guides have been recognized by many ancient cultures over the years. And

160

your guide does just that: guide you, rather than tell you what to do. Mine also brings inspirational thoughts to me – dropping great ideas into my head! If you need help, just ask. My requests normally get results within 24 hours. Might yours be the same?

True-life story
Indian spirit guide

I have several angels around me; one appears with the colour green and is my guardian angel. I feel at peace when he is around, comforted. I talk to him in my head, but also out loud and in the car, and when I am alone – I don't want anyone to think I'm 'loopy'! My spirit guide is an Indian lady, who I know was my grandmother in a previous life. She is small, but very strong and wise, and she helps me when I need direction or when I am meditating and working on spiritual things and my healing work. I smell roses when she is around. My Indian spirit guide, whom I call Ananya, brings the smell of smoke with her, like a campfire smell.

Types of spirit guide

There are many different types of spirit guide, and we will look at them in greater detail later in this chapter, but some of the ones that are most frequently seen are listed below.

- **Ancestral guides:** These are guides with whom you share some sort of family history, either recent or in the ancient past. My family guides include my late father Ron, his brother Eric and sometimes, in a healing capacity, Dad and Eric's Uncle Erne, my great-uncle. Other deceased relatives visit regularly too, but these are more like family get-togethers!
- **Animal guides:** These guides are sometimes also called totems or power animals. I work with cats of all sorts. I am very attracted to jewellery and images of leopards and cougars, seeking out clothing and accessories with leopard prints on. I keep cats as pets at home too: a ginger tom (called Tigger, of course) and a black cat that looks just like a baby panther. It seems fairly obvious to me that cats are my guides. What animal symbols do you bring instinctively into your home

to decorate household items? Look around your home – you might surprise yourself.

- **Bird guides:** All birds of prey excite me too. I have loads of photographs of myself with owls, and I also love parrots and eagles. Many people work with birds as guides or use symbols of their energy.
- **Ascended masters:** High-level advanced souls like Jesus, Mary, Krishna and Buddha are sometimes known as ascended masters. These types of guide may come to you on specific occasions rather than work with you all the time.
- **'Alien' guides:** Guides from other dimensions and realms are commonly working with human souls at this time in history, and the more advanced human souls are connecting with them (I doubt that any such friends you might have would admit to this).
- **Angel guides**: If you are reading this book, you are already working with your angel guides.
- **Nature spirits/faerie guides:** Some people are more attuned to nature spirits or faeries and believe the unseen beings of this realm are actually nature itself. Few people connect to this realm, but the ones who do are usually people who prefer to be outdoors and feel more at peace when they are in nature. If you feel a connection to the faerie or nature realms and want to draw them close to your own world there are lots of things you can do. Request that connection during meditation, speak to them on your nature walks and bring faerie-symbols and figurines into your home.

Angel blessing

Human souls are lucky enough to have many helpers here on Earth. If you want your guides to bring you signs that they are working with you, just ask that they indicate their presence when they are around. Your sign may come as a coincidence, an inspirational thought or a dream visit. Look out for other indications too.

Meeting your guides and angels in a dream

Your angels and spirit guides will already be working around you in subtle ways, but I am most comfortable when my own guides appear in dream visits. Ways to ask your guides and angels for their help in dream visits include the following:

- Record your request on a recording device: 'Angels and guides, I would love it if you would appear to me in a dream visit ... ' Simply chat away to them as you might to an old friend. (After a night's sleep you might want to check the recording, in case they also leave you a message this way.)
- Write your request in a notebook and leave it by the bed.
- Talk to a friend about how you would like your guides to appear in dreams, and ask your friend if this is something they would like too – maybe you'll both have a visit.

- Place an angel crystal (of your choice) under your pillow, or leave a handwritten request under it.
- Take an angel figurine into your bedroom and hold it before you go to bed.

Angel blessing

Allow your angels and guides to inspire you with positive thoughts and ideas. Remain open to their wisdom and guidance.

Deceased relatives as guides

Sometimes when deceased relatives appear to you after they have passed on, it's because they are appearing as a guide. It is easier to connect with a voice or vision when you're dealing with a familiar sound or face. That great-aunt with a loud, opinionated voice might come back to you with much the same personality as she had on Earth, although her 'words of wisdom' may be little different from those she gave when she lived on this side of life. However, if she hated your partner when she was alive, she'll probably still dislike him or her now that she has passed over. Use your instinct when taking advice from the Other Side, especially if it comes from someone whose advice you wouldn't have taken when they were on this side of life!

Warnings are always worth paying attention to, though. Even if Grandma is making a single visit, if she seems anxious it's probably worth paying heed to what she is saying or indicating – why else would she have crossed boundaries of time and dimension to meet you?

Some of my deceased relatives are already quite high-ranking spirits and have brought all sorts of communication with them when they've visited – in dreams, visits and other forms of contact. These include:

- Bringing a warning of a future illness and how to handle it
- Showing that they were going to be around for important future events

- Indicating that a relative should no longer grieve for them
- Sharing the love they still have for relatives on this side of life (probably the most common reason to visit)
- Checking out people and places on our behalf
- Bringing reassurance that everything will be okay

When my relatives appear in dreams their visits are clear and precise. They come to me in their human form (varying in age and appearance slightly) and I hear them speak to me in my mind, using a type of telepathy. Thousands of people have shared this type of experience with me over the years.

Aliens (off-world visitors) as guides

Many of the alien races that communicate with human souls cannot contact us in the same easy way that our deceased loved ones can. They don't use human language, but do seem able to indicate ideas and bring us feelings of reassurance that calm us when they visit. Alien guides reach out using a type of telepathy (as above), but we find it hard to translate their communication into words, even though we understand the meanings of their thoughts. Trying to describe the experience to others is almost impossible (sometimes for good reason – we're not always meant to share it).

Sometimes 'alien' guides indicate to humans that we are part of their race and have incarnated on Earth to learn about the world here. This can be frightening at first, because when we enter Earth's realms we have an instant 'veil of forgetfulness' – we simply forget who we originally were and why we are here. We can quite literally be 'them' – we are the aliens! We can be part of otherworld races. Have you ever felt that you don't quite 'fit' here or feel lonely on planet Earth? Perhaps this is why!

Know that you are on Earth for a reason and, although those reasons vary a lot, on page 167 are the mostcommon ones (I have no doubt that if you fit into one of these groups you'll feel that these suggestions move you in some way).

- **Fact-finding:** You're here on a fact-finding mission. What is Earth like? What are the people like? How can your 'home' planet learn from humans on Earth? Know that you are not alone, and you are constantly in touch with your loved ones from other worlds, even if you're not aware of it. Complete your mission with good grace, fun and love.
- **Teaching:** You've come to help the humans on Earth by teaching the wisdom of kindness, tolerance and love, among other things. The easiest way to teach these things is to be them. Alternatively, you may be a teacher of spiritual knowledge and share your truth by giving talks, running workshops or writing books).
- **Light beacon:** Your 'race' may be holding high-level energies of light around the Earth. You may feel the need to travel extensively – know that everywhere you go you leave a beacon of light behind you. Make friends with the people you meet. Relax and be friendly, to leave the highest possible light behind. Make people say, 'What a great person that was, I am so glad I met them … '

There may be other signs that you don't quite fit here:

- You have many allergies: human foods often make you ill. Solution: eat as many organic fruits and vegetables as you can; the less processed and 'messed-about' your food is, the better.
- You (or your children) find it hard to fit into traditional Earth teachings or regimes. Solution: look for jobs or teachers that are more fluid in their approach. Follow your guidance and connect to an artistic, musical or creative path – that is why you're here.
- Wars, hatred, arguments – all these things affect you very badly on a physical level. Solution: avoid watching the news, and stay away from people or situations that might cause conflict.
- Your cluttered home makes you feel stressed much of the time. Solution: sell, give away or pass on to a charity items that you no longer need. Can you move to the sea or the countryside and live a simpler life? More 'things' do not equal greater happiness!

Animal and bird guides

There are whole books dedicated to animal guides and their meanings, but it's fairly easy to work out the attributes of different types of creature. For example, dogs are used by humans as companions; they are loyal and they protect us.

Here are a few other examples to get you thinking:

- The wolf teaches us about spirituality and sacredness.
- The eagle brings us sharp vision and clarity.
- The bear respects natural cycles, reminding us that there is a time for work and a time for play.
- The owl, wise and knowing, teaches us to open our eyes and look around us.
- The horse is powerful and has great stamina, showing freedom and power and granting us safe passage.
- The dolphin shows us how to move forward with grace in our lives and find harmony in all things.
- The rabbit is timid and fearful, but willing to face its fears; it listens to its surroundings and watches out for danger.
- The butterfly happily changes from one form to emerge into the beauty of another.

What animals are you attracted to? Look for the clues all around you.

True-life story
Remembering my guide's name

I work with many different guides and angels. Some I am very aware of, as they make themselves known to me by appearing in my dreams. Others are more discreet and stand back, keeping a distance between us, but I still know they help me.

A psychic drew a picture of a nun and told me that she was one of my guides, and another artist painted me a picture of an angel with dark hair and piercing blue eyes. When I hold the painting her name immediately pops into my head (but it's only for the two of us to know). When others ask me her name, I immediately forget.

Ascended masters as guides

These high-level beings are most likely to be serving us in our accession towards the realms of light and love, rather than working on our human path. They hold positions of great responsibility, overseeing the Earth and its growth, or they work on a cosmic level. The ascended masters are part of a group called the Great White Brotherhood (the 'White' refers to the aura or halo of white light that surrounds them). They work on bringing humankind into a state of awareness – awareness that we are spiritual beings living a human life. Souls that were formed as a spark of the divine, we are just a drop of light from our living Creator God!

Faerie guides

Faeries or nature spirits are really the angels of the natural world. They are watched over by the great Archangel Ariel. I've met people who've confided in me that they feel they are part of this realm and more connected to this energetic space than they are to their human bodies. More and more people are feeling their true nature. If you feel connected to the faerie realms you probably prefer a more natural life and spend as much time out in nature as you can.

Some women I've met at conferences and shows wear faerie garments at every opportunity, including rubber pointed faerie ears and loose-flowing multicoloured skirts (often in natural fabrics), usually decorated with flowers and ribbons as well as lots of glitter! They are the most fun people, who love nothing more than dancing and singing. If you have a connection to these realms you'll understand this feeling. Meditation is a great way of connecting to these other dimensions.

The main reason that faerie guides are working with human souls at the moment is to encourage us to take care of our planet. They are concerned about litter, mining and the lack of recycling, and worry about areas of disaster caused by human intervention. My own guides have made major suggestions about recycling (an area where I was a little lazy at one point), and I now work much harder at this than I did previously: taking bags of cardboard waste to the local refuse dump where it's recycled, unwanted clothes to charity shops, and so on. How can you help? Make a list of areas that you could change for the better.

Exercise

Connect to your faerie guide

If you want to connect to this realm, find a comfortable and secluded spot in nature (even an area in your own garden can work – especially if it's left to grow a little wild).

1 Sit on a rug or a garden seat, close your eyes and take three deep breaths in through your nose, then blow it out noisily through your mouth. Allow your mind to float away in a daydream … Drift … drift …

2 Imagine a faerie being walking towards you through the undergrowth. Bow your head slightly as a sign of respect.

3 Do not attempt to touch your faerie friend, but ask him or her how you might be of service to the natural realms. Your answer may come to you as a set of images rather than words. Ask questions, if you wish.

4 When you've finished your conversation, bow your head again.

5 You can leave a little gift for your faerie guide as a symbol of energy exchange. This could be a pretty nut, a shell or a pebble, or you might leave a small coin. Other faerie gifts include mead, honey, cream and butter (best placed on half a nutshell or an

open seashell). The faerie guide will take the essence of the gift rather than the gift itself (so beware of ants and wasps!). Alternatively you can hang a piece of inexpensive jewellery on a nearby tree.

True-life story
Seeing nature spirits

When my husband and I were on holiday in Lanzarote we went on a coach trip around the volcano and, despite there being no plant life there (it was completely barren, with mounds of volcanic rock), I sat watching little nature 'beings' running around!

I am finding an ever-strengthening relationship with my guides, angels and faeries, and at times feel very strongly about causes and want to speak out to people. Because of that, situations seem to be arising where I am getting opportunities to make a difference, which I would love to be able to do.

With the faeries, I can see them physically and in my mind's eye; they are far more direct in what they do and say than angels are. With the nature spirits, I quite often smell scents when they are around – for example, fresh grass or just fresh sweet air or sea water.

Building a relationship with your guides

As with your guardian angel, your guide is ready, willing and able to connect with you. You just need to show that you are ready too. Here are a few more ideas to help you connect to your guides.

Pictures

Find, draw, paint or create an image to represent what your guide means to you. Maybe an artist friend would sketch something, following your description. Perhaps you'll find an image on the internet that reminds you of your guide, or what you'd like your guide to look like (if you haven't actually seen it). Or you might find a psychic artist who would be prepared to sketch your guide for you – try mind/body/spirit fairs for an artist who specializes in this type of work. Frame your image or keep it in a safe place.

Meditations

Sit quietly several times a week and see if you can tune into your guides. Ask them to come to you with words of advice and guidance.

Overall the best way to connect with, and become closer to, all of your guides and angels is to keep talking to them. Do this in your head, out loud or however you feel most comfortable. Write to them, ask them to appear in dreams and generally communicate your thoughts and feelings. If you need help, then ask for it – it really can be that simple. You can bring in specific guides or angels or simply ask that the best guide step forward. Watch out for those coincidental meetings with like-minded friends; or, like my danburite-crystal encounter, the answer may appear after putting out a request. Just expect the magic to be a part of your life and it will be.

Write down, or record on your computer, every special angel/guide experience that you have. It's easy to say that 'nothing' happens to us, when miraculous things may be occurring every single day in our lives – we just forget! Value your angel encounters by keeping a record of them. When you're feeling sad or alone, you can look back on the joys in your life.

When you sleep we can draw closer to you. Take note of our communication during this time, to guide you when you are awake.

Angel rituals

We, your angels, are ready to bring a little magic into your lives

Your guardian angel is always in your life and always close to you. Sadly, we are usually so switched off from the spiritual world that we are completely unaware of the mystical realms around us. It's okay just to know that the angels are in your life, but if you want to feel the magic of the angels around you, you need to consciously create the setting in which this might happen. You can easily do this using angel rituals.

What is a ritual?

A ritual is a symbolic set of actions. Rituals and ceremonies are performed for many religious reasons and to mark special occasions: lighting and then blowing out the candles on a birthday cake or wearing special clothes to a wedding are two such examples. With angel rituals you can create your own 'special occasion' rituals – and this time you make the rules.

Your ritual can be performed for a specific reason, such as asking the angels to help with healing, or just to thank the angels. Or perhaps it is performed as an acknowledgement that the angels are in your life. Your sacred rite can be performed daily, weekly, monthly or just when the occasion arises. In years gone by, these ceremonies included all sorts

> ## *Angel blessing*
>
> *Angels love to work with our fun rituals and affirmations. They understand how these act as confirmation for us, and how they help our connection with the angelic realms to grow stronger.*

of special elements, such as eating particular types of food, consuming alcohol or drugs, and even animal and human sacrifice – but don't worry, the angels don't need you to do that! Your ritual simply needs to remind you of your angelic connection and to be fun, magical and, above all, memorable.

You can bring all sorts of different elements into your ritual, but first of all you need to decide where it will take place. Here are a few examples, but no doubt you'll have your own ideas:

- An outdoor setting, such as a pretty garden or a secluded wooded area (perfect for summer rituals)
- A room at home where you usually relax
- A hall or space rented for a meeting, where you can perform the ritual with others
- A corner of a room at home where you can 'borrow' space, placing objects on display and then tidying them away afterwards

Your basic ritual kit

What sort of items will you need? It's easy to gather a basic kit together and then build on it as time and money permit. You can use inherited items, or things bought new or from end-of-season sales. Look for second-hand (resale) items too. I've picked up all sorts of pretty items from charity sales very cheaply, including candleholders and bells and antique angel-related items – they're a great place to buy angel figurines and angel-decorated gifts. However, some of the best pieces will probably be those that you make yourself.

Angel blessing

Nature's own scents are wonderful: freshly mown grass, pinecones and spring's new blooms. Scent is the surest way of recalling a long-lost memory. On days when you are especially happy, create a memory-scent to go with your feelings of peace and contentment. Display favourite flowers, wear a particular scent, or create your own sprays to wear on your person or to mist around your rooms. Tie the scent and the memory together forever in your mind, so that you can recapture that memory or feeling at any time by releasing the perfume that you've associated with it.

Exercise

Make angel-essence room sprays

Angels, it is said, arrive on a cloud of perfume. Some say this celestial scene is created from heavenly blossoms and exotic blooms; others that the angels bring our favourite flower scents with them, to relax us and bring us to peace. Descriptions include the scent of roses, gardenias, lilies, violets and even vanilla. It's easy to create this most angelic of atmospheres by making your own angel-essence room sprays.

1 First, you need a small spray bottle, so that you can spray your finished product around the room. Supermarkets and chemists sell small plastic bottles with a spray attachment (you'll find them in the travel section, along with small pots for travel-size portions of your usual creams and lotions); you can also buy glass bottles from specialist suppliers over the internet. If you order aromatherapy oils in this way you will probably be able to purchase suitable bottles from your normal supplier.

2 Start with a base of spring water and add a few drops of your favourite aromatherapy oils.* Aromatherapy oils are often called 'essential oils' and are created, usually by distillation, from the leaves, stems, flowers, bark, roots or other elements of a plant. You need just a few drops of aromatherapy oil (see below) to one cup of water. If you like, you can prepare your water by standing some crystals in it for a few hours beforehand: try rose quartz, clear quartz or amethyst. Only mix up enough solution to last you a few days (make up fresh batches as you need them). You can design your own combinations or try one or two of the 'recipes' below:

- Relaxing: 4 drops of lavender oil
- Cleansing and purifying: 2–4 drops of lemongrass oil
- Happiness and joy: 3–4 drops of orange oil
- Space-clearing: 3 drops of pine oil
- Angel invitation: 2 drops of frankincense oil

3 Pour the mixture into your spray bottle and spray your room with your angel essence whenever you wish to bring a touch of the angels' presence into your life.

* Caution: Not all aromatherapy oils are suitable for this process, so do check before you begin. It's worth sourcing a really good aromatherapy book so that you have a sound idea of which oils are suitable for which processes. Keep all oils away from the skin, and out of the reach of children and animals.

Candle power

Candles are used in rituals, magic and ceremonies all over the world. Light a candle and you are ritualistically bringing 'light' to your situation, and are working with the highest of intent – the angelic realms, the realms of light-energy.

White candles are always appropriate, but if you wish to incorporate colour into your ceremony or to enhance your 'intent', why not try using candles of different colours?

Each colour has traditional meanings and associations. Work with one colour at a time. You can even copy out these colours and their meanings into your angel notebook:

- White: truth, purity, peace (you can use white in place of all colours)
- Red: love, health, sex, strength, romance
- Green: money, luck, fertility
- Black: negativity, confusion, banishing or removing something
- Brown: uncertainty, hesitation, grounding yourself
- Pink: love, morality, honour, friendship or family
- Purple: power, business progress, ambition, psychic ability
- Orange: attraction, stimulation, happiness, children
- Blue: tranquillity, patience, health and healing

You can use the colours shown above, but if you have your own association or feel that a different colour will work with your purpose, by all means use your intuition to guide you.

Exercise

Create your own ritual using a candle

1 Prepare your space by burning incense or aromatherapy oils.

2 Ask your angels to be with you.

3 Play some relaxing 'angel music' and light a candle.

4 Say a few positive words (use phrases taken from angel cards or make up your own).

5 Perform your task, which might be:
- Meditating
- Writing a message to your angels or filling in your angel journal
- Asking questions of your angels
- Using angel cards

6 At the end of your ritual, blow out your candle and thank your angels for their help.

Crystals and their energies

Crystals have always been used to perform rituals, ceremonies and magic. They have an energy all their own, and each type of crystal has its own energetic vibration. Some have gentle energy and are wonderful for comforting you; others make you feel peaceful; and so on. Here are a few of the more easily obtainable crystals and their meanings:

Crystal	Association
Rose quartz	Unconditional love, family love, romance
Clear quartz	A 'charger' crystal that helps to enhance the power of other crystals; useful for meditation and healing
Amethyst	Traditionally used for psychic development and spiritual issues
Agate	Good health and fortune
Amber	Wealth and happiness
Citrine	Helps in challenging situations
Jasper	Inspires confidence and aids psychic development
Lapis lazuli	Success and cooperation
Moonstone	All womanly issues
Tiger's eye	Stress and pain relief

Working with crystals to perform angel magic

One of the simplest ways of using crystals for angel rituals is to hold one in the palm of your hand while meditating. Alternatively, try adding one or two crystals to your angel display, or pop them in the top of a plant pot, especially if you're growing something from seed or a cutting. You can also put a crystal under your pillow at night.

It can take time to build up a collection, but I have put the most important three crystals at the top of the table: rose quartz, clear quartz and amethyst cover most eventualities. Clear quartz can be used in place of most of the other crystals.

Small pieces of crystal work just as well as big ones. I have a large selection around my home because I love the look and feel of them. Small tumbled crystals are fairly cheap to buy, and I mix up all the colours in open bowls. I like to have them close by me when I'm working, so that I can lay them on the desk and make patterns with them – it's a very calming thing to do.

As well as placing a few crystals in between other objects on your angel display, why not create a crystal water feature (see page 71)? Or a small plug-in household waterfall would be lovely with some sparkling crystals under the water and around the display. If you don't have one of these, why not place a few crystals in a bowl of water (a cut-glass bowl would look wonderful)? You can even put a few floating candles on top. Anything that uses water needs to be kept scrupulously clean, for hygiene reasons (it will soon smell otherwise), so change the water every couple of days and scrub any residue left inside the bowl once a week. I once managed to pick up some angels that sit on the side of plant pots (from a garden centre one Christmas), so I add a little angel to the side of my bowl to complete the effect.

Another idea is to fill a shallow pottery bowl with sand and arrange your crystals in it – a bit like a mini-landscape. Be careful if you have cats, though (if you have cats, I don't need to explain this; if you don't, it doesn't matter!). Place your arrangement on your angel altar.

I also have some divided plastic boxes, where I store small crystals according to colour. Some crystal healers think you shouldn't mix up different types of crystal, but I believe that you should work with your magical stones in whatever way feels right to you – and sometimes I just like the rainbow of colours! Remember: like candles, crystals add light as well as life to your rituals and displays.

Angel blessing

The angels wish to remind us to hold the world in wonder. Never forget that you live on a beautiful planet. If you ever stop thinking of the Earth in this way, imagine yourself looking around you with the eyes of a child.

Superstitions

Being magical, and living a magical life, is really just about holding a certain 'state of mind'. As Einstein said, 'There are only two ways to live your life. One is as though nothing is a miracle. The other is as though everything is a miracle.' You can choose to live in wonder, or not – it's up to you.

Many of us follow ancient rituals without even thinking about it. The act of blowing out candles on a birthday cake and making a wish is one of the first pieces of magic that many of us perform. It's called candle magic. Or perhaps you throw coins in a fountain or down a well, and make a wish when you do that. Superstitions of many types are followed all over the world. Here are a few more:

- **Black cats:** In some countries black cats are lucky, whereas in others they represent bad luck. So, if a black cat crosses your path, you might be in for a bad day – or a really great one! Just to be on the safe side, I actually own a black cat and I've called her 'Magik'.
- **Salt:** Do you throw salt over your shoulder if you accidentally spill it? In some parts of the world it's believed you will have bad luck if you

don't. Salt is often used in magic and rituals as a cleansing and purifying tool. You might sprinkle salt in the corners of your room or at the boundaries of your house to protect your home, for example.

- **Mirrors:** In some parts of the world you cover a mirror (and every reflective surface) after the passing of a loved one. I've known people see the reflection of the deceased, but these days the experience is often seen as comforting, as indeed it's meant to be. If you break a mirror, you're supposed to have seven years of bad luck, but I've broken a few in my time and haven't suffered.

Rituals, like magic, are a way of reinforcing a particular type of behaviour. I believe that we all create our own 'luck'. So now is the time to remind you of that important lesson: think positively and hold loving thoughts! I never believe the bad omens, but always go along with the good ones. Your 'intent' is the key, so why not make everything positive? A curse is only detrimental if you believe it to be so. If someone proposes that you'll have bad luck and you believe it, then you'll look for every little thing that goes wrong and blame it on the curse. You then attract more bad luck towards you. You are the one who makes this happen, not the person who curses you.

I like to read my horoscopes too, but again I only believe the good ones! I guess it all boils down to your state of mind: keep it 'light' ... like your angel friends.

True-life story
Requesting Michael's protection

I call on the Archangel Michael a lot and ask for his protection every night for me and my loved ones; I also ask him to be with me when I drive anywhere. The thought connection is instant, so I know I am always heard, but I always thank him too. For a deeper connection I meditate with candles and incense and ask for any information or guidance that he wishes to make me aware of.

Positive 'affirmation' rituals

Once you understand the power of positive thinking, you can make it work in your favour. By performing positive rituals each day (saying

positive things, thinking in a positive way) you begin to draw more good towards you. Asking your angels for help reminds you that you are not alone. It gives you a certain type of confidence, which you carry around. Ask your angels to help you whenever you need a little extra support.

Positive sayings are called affirmations, and you can use them to help you connect with your angels each day. The angel cards that I have designed contain many positive sayings and affirmations (look for them at your local bookshop or on the internet). This is a useful way of discovering suitable phrases that you can use in your life. Here are five that I have selected at random:

- Free your mind of all negative thoughts, for we are helping.
- God's beautiful creatures wish to work with you.
- We ask you to choose happiness today.
- Angels will inspire you to create something beautiful.
- Wherever you are in the world, an angel is by your side.

Place your angel cards in a photo-holder, peg them to a length of twine hanging from a shelf or just prop them up somewhere – anywhere you will see them throughout the day. Of course you can always make your own affirmation cards. Simply write out or print your positive angel-inspired sayings on a piece of card and decorate it, if you fancy having a go. You can use little phrases like the ones I have suggested above, or just go through the dictionary pulling out positive words that uplift and inspire you – love, peace, create, magic, happy, wish etc. Handwrite with a calligraphy pen or print from the computer.

Angel blessing

Angels are happy to work with our own personal affirmations. They encourage positive thinking and will be organizing help for you behind the scenes. They want to assist us in achieving our goals.

Other affirmation rituals

Add a positive saying to your computer background, or use it as a scrolling 'screensaver'. Your phrase might read something like this:

- We, your angels, are always by your side
- Your angels take care of your every need; know that it is done
- If you are afraid, you can call upon us
- Your angels love you unconditionally
- You are already perfect in our eyes

Alternatively, have a saying of the week or month that you write everywhere: 'I am happy … because my angels are here for me', or 'I am safe … because my angels are here for me', and so on. Whatever support you need from the angels, or whatever your biggest worry, that is how you decide on the positive saying, which you need to repeat as often as possible.

Further ideas for rituals

Each morning, before I start work in my angel room/study, I like to cleanse the room 'energetically'. I spritz the air in the room with 'angel-essence spray'. I particularly like to use the ones created by angel expert Hazel Raven and, as she is a friend, I am lucky enough to get them as gifts, but she also sells them on the internet. Various other people also create sprays, using spring water, aromatherapy oils and crystal 'essences'. The delicate scent of such a spray somehow changes the feel of the room and really sets me up for the day!

Don't forget that you can also make your own (see page 177).

I do a similar ritual if I've had visitors, or if someone has exchanged a cross word in my home (even if it was me!). I'll take an incense stick or joss-stick – my favourite is Nag Champa (a natural incense) – and wave it around my room, all the while imagining large angel wings sweeping the space clear using the smoke. It's great fun to dance around too; I waft the smoke up into every corner of the room, and sometimes through the whole house. Naturally it leaves the most wonderful scent.

I am lucky enough to have a special chair to meditate on at home. I sit down several times a week (if I can get the cat out of the chair) to connect with my guardian angels. I usually light a candle or two. I am fond of vanilla, if I'm using scented candles, or may light a plain unscented candle and use an aromatherapy oil burner to scent the room instead.

You can buy aromatherapy oil burners and oils all over the place: lots of gift shops stock them, as do health-food stores and New Age shops. You simply pour water into the dish or well on the top, then put in a few drops of aromatherapy oil, before lighting a candle underneath – the scent (and energy) of the oil infuses your room, changing the smell as well as the feel of your space. Do ensure that the oil you pick is safe to use in this way (ask in the shop). When working with angels I normally use three drops of one of the following: lavender, rose, frankincense, rosemary or geranium. Do not let the water run dry or it will damage your oil burner.

If your oil burner has a glass bowl on top, only add warm water to 'top up', because if you add cold water to the hot glass it will break. I've done this by mistake a couple of times, although nothing goes to waste; as I mentioned earlier, leftover angel stands (everything is decorated with angels in my house) are great for holding the larger crystal balls that I collect.

Use the ideas in this chapter as a starting point, and consider how you can create your own rituals. How can you bring a little magic into your life by performing regular actions to bless the seasons, welcome new pets or cleanse your home? Make a note of everything you do, and of your thoughts and feelings concerning each action, as well as recording how the ritual helped you.

We love to perform rituals and create magic with you. We know it is a way of connecting more closely with our human friends.

Angel blessing scrolls

Write your words and we will help them manifest into reality for you

The ancients sent messages to their guardians and guides using smoke, rocks, wood, leaves and writing on cave walls. They also looked for messages in everything from cloud movements to the shapes formed by animal entrails. These days we're more likely to communicate with our guardian angels using angel cards, but there is no reason why we can't re-create some of the traditional ways to new effect (not with animal entrails perhaps!).

One of the loveliest ways is by creating blessing scrolls – beautifully inscribed messages or requests written in the time-honoured way on paper, which can either be kept as a special memento or presented to someone as a gift.

The famous Dead Sea Scrolls

If you recall anything from your school history lessons, you'll probably know that the oldest books were written as scrolls. Between 1947 and 1956 a series of ancient scrolls were discovered in 11 caves along the north-west shore of the Dead Sea. The first scrolls were found by a Bedouin shepherd boy and his cousin. The story goes that the young boy was throwing small stones into the cave to drive out an animal when

the stone hit the side of one of the pottery jars in which the scrolls had been stored. Going into the cave to investigate, he discovered the first of the scrolls.

The 'Dead Sea Scrolls', as they became known, were found in an area 21 km (13 miles) east of Jerusalem; 396 m (1,300 ft) below sea level. The 972 texts, mostly fragmented now, are numbered according to the cave in which they were found. They are the greatest manuscript discovery of modern times.

What is fascinating about the scrolls is that many of them contain fragments of the Old Testament. Naturally this helps to date the scrolls, which contain missing pages from the Bible. Several prophecies by Ezekiel, Jeremiah and Daniel that are not included in the Bible are found in the scrolls.

These ancient scrolls contained important information for their peoples and were recorded in many ways, including writing on animal skins and papyrus. Some of the scrolls were made of copper and were inscribed using a carbon-based ink (the black ink was iron-gall ink and the red ink was cinnabar); or powdered charcoal, which was easy to erase.

The 'words' were written from right to left. Little punctuation was used, and in some cases there were no spaces between the words. This has made translation difficult, but some of the scrolls have been translated and are available to read on the internet. Many of the scrolls are yellowish or brown in colour, but some of the finest are almost white.

I did some research into the 'paper', because I was fascinated by the care that was taken in choosing the materials to write on. The scrolls that are written on animal skin are believed to have been treated with salt and flour to remove the hair, and then tanned with 'gall-nut' liquid that was brushed or sprinkled over the surface of the skin. Some scrolls were literally stitched together to form long lengths.

The scrolls were written in these languages, namely Hebrew, Aramaic and Greek. They were important documents and were hidden for many years, for safekeeping. The Temple Scroll is the longest at 8.8 m (29 ft). But the copper scrolls are among the most intriguing, as they list sites of hidden treasure! The scrolls are believed to be the library of the ancient Jewish sect known as the Essenes.

How the scrolls were protected

What else have we learnt about these early scrolls? Numerous scrolls were wrapped in linen rags; this seems to have protected them in an extraordinary way over the years, and even though they were found in a fragile condition it has still been possible to read many of them. High-quality photographs have helped us keep a record of them, after some of the pieces began to disintegrate once they were handled.

Other scrolls were found in pottery jars (with lids) around 55 cm (21½ in) in height. The dry area in which they were found meant that wooden and pottery fragments from that era have also survived into modern times, giving us a unique insight into the way people lived then. The scrolls themselves were left undisturbed for at least 1,900 years. They were precious documents, treated with care and created to hold important and long-lasting records that people could read many years in the future.

Ancient books

The same could be said of the oldest books. Ancient books like the Bible were always written by hand, long before the printing press had been invented. Books could take many years to write and were owned only by the very rich.

Fancy scripts were a beauty to behold, but the books were often illustrated too. The first letter of a section of writing would frequently be turned into an artwork in itself, and was usually shown considerably larger than the other letters on the page. Precious gold leaf may even have been used to embellish the images and enhance the writing; this was especially true when the books were religious texts, like the Bible. We can learn from this and use similar techniques to illustrate our very own blessing scrolls.

Blessing scrolls

In ancient times messages to the angels, gods and higher beings were created out of rune stones (magical symbols drawn on small rocks or carved into wood; or written on leaves, bark and even leather). When we look at the example of the Dead Sea Scrolls – those most important of ancient records – we realize how they were cared for with great reverence and we can immediately see why they were protected. They were precious, probably moved to the caves at some time for safekeeping, and split between various places so that if some were found others would still be safe. Blessing scrolls seem to have had their origins in ancient Egypt, although the Celts and Druids also used them. You can make your own scrolls and fill them with blessings, wishes and even spells! Let's look at a few ideas:

- Create something on special, good-quality paper (gold, silver or hand-pressed papers would be brilliant).
- You can handwrite your own scrolls using beautiful calligraphy or print interesting fonts on your computer. Borrow a book from the library and have a go at copying some of the old scripts.
- Illustrations would be a lovely addition: paint or draw them straight on to the page to enhance your words, or add images from magazines, or glue pictures on to the page afterwards.
- Once the scrolls are complete, they can be rolled in the traditional way and tied with string, ribbon, leather thongs or strips of silk.
- The scrolls may either be kept or presented to someone as a gift.
- You might decide to store them in a pottery jar (like the Dead Sea Scrolls) or in a wooden box.
- Alternatively, you could wrap your scroll in linen (or perhaps cotton) in the traditional way, or roll them inside a hand-decorated silk scarf.

I think it's a shame to hide blessing scrolls away, so it would be lovely to create your scroll with special words as a gift and then frame it, so that

it can be hung on a wall for everyone to see. This is a modern way of protecting and preserving your magical texts.

The purpose of your scroll

If you decide to create your own blessing scroll, you'll need time to make it properly, as in the ancient traditions, and you'll want to make sure that your finished scroll is a piece of art. Above all, it's important to determine your purpose or reason for creating it. Your scroll might serve many purposes, including:

- Requests of your angels or higher beings
- Giving thanks
- Prayers or other messages to God or the angels
- Positive words and phrases
- Best wishes or uplifting thoughts for the future of the owner
- A spell or ritual

Exercise
Create your scroll message

1 If the scroll is being made as a gift, include the new owner's name at the top of your work. Begin with a phrase such as: 'The angels ... (or insert a specific angel's name here) bless ... (add the name of the recipient).'

2 The rest of the message is yours to create, but here are a few suggestions to get you started:
- **Birth:** Your guardian angel watches over you, cares for you and protects you, standing by your side your whole life long.
- **Wedding:** May your marriage be everything you wish for, incorporating love from the angels to bless this special union.
- **New job:** May you grow in confidence and skill ...

3 If you're good at poetry, why not create a poem specifically for your scroll, or copy an existing piece of poetry that conveys your chosen meaning?

Archangels to include on blessing scrolls

You can include specific angel names as part of your blessings. Below are the archangels' traditional associations, and the types of scroll they might best be used for.

Archangel	Traditional associations	Useful for scrolls relating to:
Ariel	Animals and birds; nature kingdoms; faerie realms	Celebration of the seasons; introducing a new pet to the home or celebrating an existing pet; promoting the growth of seeds, plants and crops
Azrael	Fishermen, the sea; a crossing-over angel	Safe sea crossings; saying goodbye; the passing of a loved one
Chamuel	World peace; protection; soulmates; happiness	The safekeeping of a place or planet; finding a loved one or blessing an existing relationship
Gabriel	Communication; messenger, scribe, record-keeper	Celebration of a new book; blessing an important announcement
Haniel	The moon; female issues	Instigating feelings of love, kindness and compassion; celebrating the change from one phase of life to another (becoming a woman, becoming pregnant, the birth of a child)
Jeremiel	Psychic dreams and clairvoyance	Enhancing psychic ability; ritual scrolls
Jophiel	Creative endeavours	Manifesting or creating something

Archangel	Traditional associations	Useful for scrolls relating to:
Metatron	Keeper of the Book of Life (Akashic Records); relationships; careers	Children; celebrating relationships
Michael	Protection	Safe travel
Raguel	Resolving disagreements	Peace; celebrating happiness and success
Raphael	Healing	Celebrations or blessings relating to positive outcomes in health matters
Raziel	Higher sciences; magic and esoteric words	Magic and rituals; Earth issues
Sandalphon	Prayer-carrying	Messages for the Creator; giving thanks
Sariel	Guardianship; children's spirits	Pregnancy and childbirth
Uriel	Earth and earth healing; healing medicines	Care of the planet (see also Raphael)
Zadkiel	Forgiveness; comfort	Mending relationships; bringing peace to challenging situations

Exercise
Mini angel blessing scrolls

How about creating some mini angel blessing scrolls?

1 Using a paper guillotine, or cutting ragged edges using a pair of sharp-edged craft scissors, cut out small scrolls of paper.

2 Now write your special messages with gold or silver pens. See the suggested wordings below for some examples.

3 Roll the paper into scrolls and secure them using gold or silver twine (available from craft shops) or curling gift ribbon. Alternatively, use tiny elastic hair bands or tie the scrolls with coloured embroidery thread.

4 Place the scrolls in a basket so that people can select one each as a gift at:
- Healing sessions or psychic readings
- Religious festivals such as christenings, bar mitzvahs, weddings, and so on
- Table settings at family gatherings

Alternatively, add them to wrapped gifts or secure them to the outside of greetings cards (or in place of greetings cards).

Suggested wording for mini blessing scrolls

All scrolls can begin with the phrase: 'The angels bring this message of joy'

Followed by one of the following:

- Blessed be this child
- You are loved
- You are always protected
- We are watching over your loved ones
- We are with you

- We watch over your personal belongings
- Know that we are helping your situation
- Animals on Earth are your dear friends and companions
- Nature is your special place of contemplation
- Angels are helping with your earthly needs

Make angels a part of your life

It's always sad when you reach the end of a book that you've enjoyed. However, you can easily use this book as a reference to look at time and again. Dip in and select a page at random when you need a little angel inspiration. Remember always to watch out for your angel signs, and find new ways of making them a part of your life each and every day. Never forget to call upon your angels every time you feel lonely, sad or afraid, and to thank them each time they make their presence known.

True-life story
Recognizing the Archangel Michael

My middle daughter is very open to other realities. One day she described seeing a male angel; she said he was tall and was dressed like a warrior with a sword. She has never seen any drawings or photos of the Archangel Michael, but her description immediately reminded me of him. Another day when I was reading my angel cards she spotted a picture of the Archangel Michael and immediately pointed to the cards and said, 'Mummy, that's the angel I saw!'

We, your angels, adore, support and protect you. Never forget that we love you, exactly as you are right now.

Index

Acknowledgements

Author's acknowledgements
A big thank you to everyone at my publisher for helping me to turn the vision in my head into the beautiful book you see in front of you.

Special thanks to my wonderful fans for continuing to follow my work. I dedicate this book to you – may your angels always be by your side.

Picture acknowledgements
All photography © Octopus Publishing Group/Polly Wreford: except for page 7 and repeats Alexander Potapov/Fotolia; page 8 and repeats Pixel & Création/Fotolia; page 10 and repeats arthurdent/Fotolia; page 16 and repeats Alois/Fotolia; page 26 and repeats Marina Lohrbach/Fotolia.

Publisher's acknowledgements
With thanks to Rockett St George for the loan of some of the beautiful jewellery and props (www.rockettstgeorge.co.uk).

Commissioning Editor: **Liz Dean**
Managing Editor: **Clare Churly**
Art Director: **Jonathan Christie**
Art Direction and Design: **Tracy Killick**
Photographer: **Polly Wreford**
Stylist: **Catherine Woram**
Model: **Louise Dainton at MOT Models**
Production Manager: **Katherine Hockley**